# The Philosopher and the Storyteller

*Charles R. Embry*

# THE PHILOSOPHER AND THE STORYTELLER

## ERIC VOEGELIN AND TWENTIETH-CENTURY LITERATURE

UNIVERSITY OF
MISSOURI PRESS
COLUMBIA

Copyright © 2008 by
The Curators of the University of Missouri
University of Missouri Press, Columbia, Missouri 65211
Printed and bound in the United States of America
All rights reserved
First paperback printing, 2018


Library of Congress Cataloging-in-Publication Data

Embry, Charles R., 1942–
  The philosopher and the storyteller : Eric Voegelin and twentieth-
century literature / Charles R. Embry.
      p. cm.
  Includes bibliographical references and index.
  ISBN  978-0-8262-2152-0
  1. Literature—Philosophy. 2. Literature—History and criticism—
Theory, etc. 3. Voegelin, Eric, 1901-1985—Criticism and interpretation.
4. Literature—20th century—History and criticism. I. Title.
  PN49.E516 2008
  809'.04—dc22
                                                2007051053


♾™ This paper meets the requirements of the American National Standard
for Permanence of Paper for Printed Library Materials, Z39.48, 1984.


*Typeface: Minion*

Publication of this book has been assisted by a contribution from the Eric
Voegelin Institute, which gratefully acknowledges the generous support
provided for the series by the Earhart Foundation and the Sidney Richards
Moore Memorial Fund.

For credits, see p. 191.

TO MY CHILDREN:
MATTHEW, MEREDITH, AND PATRICK

The story was saved and not lost and it would save us, if we would be guided by it.

~ PLATO

---

# CONTENTS

## ACKNOWLEDGMENTS

I owe the largest debt for this study to a man I never met and with whom I never spoke. That man was Robert B. Heilman, who as the friend, correspondent, and "native informant" (as he thought of his own relation to Voegelin) provided Voegelin countless occasions for reflections on literature. Heilman's own literary criticism, as well as his gentle probing and questioning of Voegelin's responses to that criticism, stimulated Voegelin to reflect explicitly upon literature and its philosophical dimensions. Moreover, Voegelin trusted to his friend Bob Heilman's literary judgment the vetting of his writing in one of the most significant of his theoretical statements, namely, what would become the introduction to Voegelin's *Order and History*. So, in a very real sense, owing the origins and, to a large extent, the form of this study to Robert B. Heilman and his correspondence with Voegelin, I acknowledge that debt. Because of Bob's health at the time of my work on the correspondence, his son, Pete, happily granted permission to publish Bob's letters, and I acknowledge here my debt to Pete Heilman not only for his permission to publish the letters, but also for his enthusiastic early support of the project, his friendship, and his abiding interest in the present work—stimulated in part as it is by Bob's correspondence with Eric.

Without the support of Ellis Sandoz, Tim Hoye, Chip Hughes, Beverly Jarrett, and Polly Detels, the shape and content of this work could not have formed as it did. I have Ellis Sandoz to thank for introducing me to the excitement of philosophy and the work of Voegelin as well as his continuing support of my work. To my friend and colleague Tim Hoye, I owe thanks for many years of stimulating and far-ranging philosophical and political conversation. To my friend and colleague Chip Hughes, I am grateful for his generous support of my work on this project and for many long philosophical conversations deep into the night. I am also very grateful to Beverly Jarrett for her early belief in the project and for her continuing support of it. When I first mentioned the idea to her, she promptly wrote it down in her little spiral notebook—*with a deadline!* Thank you, Bev. Without my wife Polly's faith in me and the project itself, as well as the conversations we have conducted throughout the years about Voegelin and literature, this book would not have seen the light. Polly read and critiqued drafts at every stage of the process.

The specific work on this book began when I was granted a Faculty Development Leave for the fall semester 2004, and I acknowledge here the invaluable support that this leave provided me for reading and reflection. I hereby express my thanks and gratitude for their support of my work to the members of the Faculty Development Committee, Provost Joyce Scott, and President Keith McFarland at Texas A&M University–Commerce. I thank also Dean of Arts and Sciences Jim Klein for his support of my work through the approval of load reductions, travel support for attendance and participation in professional conferences, and monetary help with the acquiring of permissions. Most important, I would like to thank Paul Lenchner, my department head and friend of many years, for his generous support not only on this project but for numerous projects throughout the years.

Nancy Davis Bray, Flannery O'Connor Collection, Ina Dillard Russell Library, Georgia College & State University, and Scott Downing, director of interlibrary loans, Gee Library, Texas A&M University–Commerce, generously and expeditiously helped me locate materials when I needed them.

To Jane Lago, managing editor, University of Missouri Press, Julie Schorfheide, my copyeditor, and Julianna Schroeder, my guide through the process of turning the manuscript into a book at the Press, I express my sincere gratitude and thanks for their timely advice and for saving me from my own most egregious errors.

I also acknowledge a debt for provocative and stimulating conversations to Everett Zimmerman and the participants in the National Endowment for the Humanities Summer Seminar—"Eighteenth Century Historiography and Fiction"—held at the University of California, Santa Barbara, in 1993. It was during this seminar that I began work on *The Demons.*

Finally, I thank the Earhart Foundation for a Fellowship Research Grant that provided financial support for a six-month period during which I was able to complete the manuscript. I am deeply grateful for their support.

# Abbreviations of Works Cited in the Text

AFIL    Charles R. Embry, ed., *Robert B. Heilman and Eric Voegelin: A Friendship in Letters, 1944–1984*

Ds    Heimito von Doderer, *The Demons*

TVBIA    Flannery O'Connor, *The Violent Bear It Away*

W    Graham Swift, *Waterland*

# THE
# PHILOSOPHER
# AND THE
# STORYTELLER

# "Composed of Wonders"

## Literature of the Spirit

We shall not come home to the facts of our unhousedness, of our eviction from a central humanity in the face of the tidal provocations of political barbarism and technocratic servitude, if we do not redefine, if we do not re-experience, the life of meaning in the text, in music, in art. We must come to recognize, and the stress is on *re*-cognition, a meaningfulness which is that of a freedom of giving and of reception beyond the constraints of immanence.　　　　～ GEORGE STEINER, *REAL PRESENCES*

Going back, way back, to the earliest times, when men and women and children looked at one another, at the land, at the sky, at rivers and oceans, at mountains and deserts, at animals and plants, and wondered, as it is in our nature to do: what is all this that I see and hear and find unfolding before me? How shall I comprehend the life that is in me and around me? To do so, stories were constructed—and told, and remembered, and handed down over time, over the generations. Some stories—of persons, of places, of events—were called factual. Some stories were called "imaginative" or "fictional": in them, words were assembled in such a way that readers were treated to a narration of events and introduced to individuals whose words and deeds . . . struck home.

　　　　～ ROBERT COLES, *THE CALL OF STORIES*

---

W orld wars hot and cold—among combatants claiming exclusive possession of truth, resulting in massive displacements of peoples, destruction of cultures, political barbarism, and genocide—characterize not only the twentieth century but the present as well. Therefore, it is apropos that we continue to ponder the work of Eric Voegelin, a philosopher who spent his lifetime exploring the nature of modernity and meditating upon the sources of order in human existence. That Voegelin's philosophy shares an essential link with literature and art underlies the justification for a work of literary criticism that focuses upon the nature of literature, its philosophical import, and the crucial importance of literature in helping address the crises of modern political, social, and spiritual disorder.[1] Modern literature can best be understood within the larger context of philosophy: as one of the symbolizations resulting from the millennial activity of human beings seeking to articulate and communicate experiences of the world, a world from which they emerge as conscious beings who bear within themselves the imaginative capacity both to experience the intangible reality that is the ground of their being and to articulate that experience through fictive language. Indeed, George Steiner recognizes that literature in particular, and art in general, lies at the heart of our attempts to understand the political barbarism of modernity and to explore avenues back into our "central humanity." Works of literature and Voegelin's philosophical work are, moreover, linked by what Robert Coles identifies as "the call of stories."[2] That human beings throughout history and in all cultures have told stories (and continue to tell stories) testifies to the need we have for stories—to tell and be told stories. Tom Crick, the history teacher-narrator of Graham Swift's *Waterland*, tells his students: "Only nature knows neither memory nor history. But man—let me offer you a definition—is the story-telling animal" (*W*, 62).

Voegelin's search of historical order in response to the political and moral disorder of his age, and the meditative search that he conducted for the source and ground of his existence and its order throughout his life, led him to understand that man is indeed a storyteller. In the section of *In Search of Order* entitled "The True Story" Voegelin writes:

> The quest for truth, it appears, does not result in a piece of information that would have been available at other times and in other situations or that, when found, would be unqualifiedly valid in its specific form for all future times in all future situations. The event of the quest is part of

1. The term *literature*, while it includes various genres, will refer primarily—unless otherwise noted—to works of fiction, and more specifically to novels. While some of the observations and assertions that are made about literature may indeed be applicable to other genres, our primary focus is on the novel.
2. Coles, *Call of Stories*.

a story told by the It, and yet a story to be told by the human questioner, if he wants to articulate the consciousness of his quest as an act of participation in the comprehending story. The "story" thus emerges as the symbolism that will express the awareness of the divine-human movement and countermovement in the quest for truth. . . . Telling a story in this metaleptic sense of the term is not a matter of choice. The story is the symbolic form the questioner has to adopt necessarily when he gives an account of his quest as the event of wresting, by the response of his human search to a divine movement, the truth of reality from a reality pregnant with truth yet unrevealed.[3]

The language of this story that is told by what Voegelin calls the It-reality, in partnership with the human questioner, is "not narratively referential but luminously symbolic."[4]

The "literature of the spirit"[5] to which the title of this prologue refers is the literature of writers who are moved to write by a vocation from which they cannot escape. It is not unrelated to earlier forms of expression and symbolization inspired by various Greek muses, forms that involve the human need and capacity to tell stories that express the human quest for understanding and meaning. The literature of the spirit is today often obscured by the exalted status accorded to objective reality and the facticity of the world of matter, and by the practical success of technological innovation, itself often confused with science, thereby tending to obscure the more profound insights into reality of modern natural science. The stories that constitute the substance of fiction are often relegated to the subjective world of entertainment and amusement. Worse, fiction has come to be associated with forms of art that are believed simply to be expressions of "personal" worldviews that speak only to those persons who share them.

Publishers regularly declare that fiction is imaginary—and, therefore, not real—by including on the copyright pages of novels the following statement, or something akin to it: "This is a work of fiction. Names, characters, places, and incidents either are the product of the author's imagination or are used fictitiously, and any resemblance to actual persons, living or dead, business establishments, events or locales

---

3. Voegelin, *In Search of Order,* 38–39. Addressing the question "Why do we write?" in his Nobel lecture, Imre Kertesz asserted that "it never occurred to me that when it came to this question, one had a choice." Kertesz, "Eureka!: The 2002 Nobel Lecture," 4.

4. Ibid., 41.

5. The term *literature of the spirit* is taken from Campbell, *The Power of Myth,* 3.

is entirely coincidental."[6] The problem with this disavowal, one that raises the question of the nature of fiction, is a theme of Tim O'Brien's novel *The Things They Carried*.[7] The disclaimer duly appears on the back of the title page and reads in full: "This is a work of fiction. Except for a few details regarding the author's own life, all the incidents, names, and characters are imaginary." O'Brien, however, muddies his disavowal by dedicating the book "to the men of Alpha Company, and in particular to Jimmy Cross, Norman Bowker, Rat Kiley, Mitchell Sanders, Henry Dobbins, and Kiowa," and subsequently filling all the stories he tells with characters named Jimmy Cross, Norman Bowker, Rat Kiley, Mitchell Sanders, Henry Dobbins, and Kiowa. What then, O'Brien provokes us to ask, is the nature and status of reality and truth in fiction?

Deadly to the literature of the spirit is a common view of novels as expressions of realities that are freely constructed in the imaginations of writers, imaginations unrestricted and unlimited by the constraints of a shared reality in which all human beings exist and participate. The imaginative freedom of novels has come to be opposed to the facticity of nonfiction and is thus presumed to be created for the amusement and diversion of readers, or for a momentary flight from the anxiety of the human condition into wished worlds of harmony and love. In other words, fiction gets a bad reputation for having nothing to say about our common humanity and everything to say about solipsistic wants, needs, quirks, or tastes of atomized individuals.

Nothing, however, seems to diminish the call that stories continue to exercise on millions of people. We continue to tell stories and listen to the stories we are told, no matter what the genre. Writing of his parents' life-long habit of reading stories aloud, Robert Coles says that "I can still remember my father's words as he tried to tell me, with patient conviction, that novels contain 'reservoirs of wisdom,' out of which he and our mother were drinking. . . . 'Your mother and I feel rescued by these books. We read them gratefully. You'll also be grateful one day to the authors.'"[8]

The understanding and reading of literature evinced herein challenges the reigning popular and academic views of imaginative literature: that

6. While this particular disavowal is taken from the copyright page of *Acqua Alta,* a police procedural novel by Donna Leon, I have noticed that it appears regularly in many contemporary novels by houses that publish for the popular mass market. See also copyright pages of Rankin, *Fleshmarket Alley,* and Francis, *Wild Horses.*
7. O'Brien, *The Things They Carried,* copyright page and dedication.
8. Coles, *Call of Stories,* xii.

novels, poems, and stories are simply expressions of "personal," subjective experiences, which have nothing to do with reality in its personal, social, spiritual, or cosmic dimensions. I exclude from my consideration those more popular genres of fiction such as mystery, science fiction, fantasy, or romance, even though these forms rely upon the same linguistic techniques as the fiction with which I am concerned. Certainly, under some conditions, works that fall within these genres symbolize and express the human search for understanding and meaning. It seems, however, that these forms are written primarily for profit and as Pascalian *divertissements* to amuse and momentarily to divert readers from the calamities and disorders of the human condition. The popularity of these forms seems to encourage the belief that fiction can only narrate unreal, "imaginative" worlds of writers' fantasies.[9] One of the most remarkable distinctions between imagination and fantasy was made by Nobel Prize–winning novelist Gabriel García Márquez. From an artist's perspective he identified the connection between reality and imagination when he was asked by a friend why he loathes fantasy and embraces the writer's imagination. "Because," García Márquez responded,

> I believe the imagination is just an instrument for producing reality and that *the source of creation is always, in the last instance, reality.* Fantasy, in the sense of pure and simple Walt-Disney-style invention without any basis in reality is the most loathsome thing of all. I remember once when I was interested in writing a book of children's stories, I sent you a draft of "The Sea of Lost Time." With your usual frankness you said you didn't like it. You thought the problem lay in your not being keen on fantasy and the argument devastated me because children don't like fantasy either. What they do like is imagination. The difference between the one and the other is the same as between a human being and a ventriloquist's dummy.[10]

The case that I will present for reading novels as contributions to the human search for order is rooted in the conviction that the literature of

9. Although I may appear to dismiss these subgenres of fiction as unimportant, I do not intend to do so, for their existence as well as their popularity testify not only to the call of stories but to a deep psychological desire either for a certainty that is not vouchsafed us as human beings (a certainty that the novelists we read here also deny us) or as escapes from the uncertainty that we experience in our lives, a desire exacerbated by the prevailing views on justice, goodness, truth, and beauty. Sometimes, indeed, escapes, at least momentary escapes, are necessary, given the mode of living that we have created in the "advanced" segments of the world.

10. Mendoza and García Márquez, *The Fragrance of Guava*, 31. Emphasis added.

the spirit—despite the fact that it is imaginative *and* fictive or even *because* it is imaginative and fictive—enables us to understand the Heraclitean "one ordered universe common (to all)."[11] Not only does this literature enable us to understand this "one ordered universe common (to all)," but without this literature it is less possible to develop and fulfill our potential as human beings. Perhaps it is not even possible, without fiction, to understand those dimensions of the reality in which we find ourselves immersed, dimensions that bestow upon us our being and permit us to discover meaning and fulfillment in our personal lives as well as in the larger environment of society and history.

While there are no hard and fast criteria by which one can decide what works fall into the category of the literature of the spirit as opposed to literature created to amuse, entertain, or divert, one characteristic that binds examples of the former into an identifiable group is their recondite complexity and their insistence that their readers engage the world as they engage the story. Early novelist innovators like Sterne and Cervantes, who probe and explore the nature of human consciousness and reality, as well as twentieth-century novelists as diverse as Faulkner, Kazantzakis, Broch, Mann, Saramago, and Péter Nádas, create works of art that require from their readers commitment, patience, time, and *especially imagination and reflection* in order to experience the depth and mystery of their stories. Milan Kundera argues that "the novel's spirit is the spirit of complexity. Every novel says to the reader: 'Things are not as simple as you think.' That is the novel's eternal truth, but it grows steadily harder to hear amid the din of easy, quick answers that come faster than the question and block it off."[12] Political theorist Hannah Arendt has also called attention to the difficulties manifested by novels and the demands they make upon their readers. In her introduction to the Universal Library edition of Hermann Broch's *Sleepwalkers*, she observes that the modern novel "confronts . . . [the reader] with problems and perplexities in which the reader must be prepared to engage himself if he is to understand it at all. The result of this transformation [of the novel] has been that the most accessible and popular art has become one of the most difficult and esoteric. . . . The intention [of novelists has become] to involve the reader in something which is at least as much a process of thought as of artistic invention."[13]

---

11. Heraclitus Fragment B89, *Ancilla*, trans. Freeman, 30. The complete fragment reads: "To those who are awake, there is one ordered universe common (to all), whereas in sleep each man turns away (from this world) to one of his own."
12. Kundera, "Depreciated Legacy of Cervantes," 18.

The complexity of modern novels stems largely from the nature of the reality (or realities) they explore. Traditionally, philosophy has been concerned with the nature of reality, a concern that was expressed in modern form by the well-known questions of Leibniz: "Why is there something, why not nothing? And, Why is the something as it is and not different?" What then is the reality that fiction symbolizes and makes present? And how is it related to the philosophy created and developed in ancient Greece as it has been continued by such thinkers as Eric Voegelin?

Milan Kundera also claims for fiction what he calls the traditional prerogative of philosophy—that of understanding being. "If it is true," he asserts, "that philosophy and science have forgotten about man's being, it emerges all the more plainly that with Cervantes a great European art took shape that is nothing other than the investigation of this forgotten being."[14] Nadine Gordimer, novelist and Nobel Laureate, confirms Kundera's assertion that modern novels explore being and quotes approvingly her fellow novelist, Nikos Kazantzakis, who wrote in *Report to Greco* that "art is the representation not of the body but of the forces which created the body."[15]

That writers and artists experience, explore, and symbolize their experiences of the forces of being, Gordimer believes, connects the art of literature and novels with myth. In her Nobel lecture, she empha-sized the continuing importance of myth in the face of its apparent replacement by the explanations of modern natural science. She observed, "There are many proven explanations for natural phenomena now; and there are new questions of being arising out of some of the answers. For this reason, the genre of myth has never been entirely abandoned, although we are inclined to think of it as archaic. . . . *The forces of being remain. They are what the writer, as distinct from the con-temporary popular mythmaker, still engage today, as myth in its ancient form attempted to do.*"[16] Refining her understanding of the writer's vocation to address and explore the forces of being that constitute real-ity, Gordimer comments that "the writer in relation to *the nature of per-ceivable reality and what is beyond—imperceivable reality*—is the basis for all . . . [literary] studies. . . . Life is aleatory in itself; being is constantly pulled and shaped this way and that by circumstances and different

13. Arendt, Introduction to *The Sleepwalkers*, by Broch, v–vi.
14. Kundera, "Depreciated Legacy of Cervantes," 4–6.
15. Gordimer, "Writing and Being," 173.
16. Ibid. Emphasis added.

levels of consciousness."[17] In the exploration of those "forces of being" and the fictional symbolizations of the human experience of these forces, Gordimer identifies the linkage between "myth in its ancient form" and the novelist. Her assertions call attention to a theme that appears throughout this study of philosophy and literature, i.e., the continuing importance and relevance of myth to human beings and the extent to which modern literature and novels are philosophically related to that ancient form of fictive literature.

While Gordimer emphasizes the nexus between myth and novels in the exploration and symbolization of "perceivable reality and what is beyond—imperceivable reality"—the forces of being, Voegelin linked myth and philosophy as equivalent forms of symbolization that express Being in flux. Voegelin calls the linguistic linkage between myth and philosophy the "Time of the Tale." The Time of the Tale as formulated by Voegelin provides a key to understanding the linguistic symbolization of the interpenetration and mutual participation of the various partners—human, cosmic, and divine—in Being. The community of Being that is symbolized by the human imagination in the linguistically imaginative Tale is, as we shall see, also imaginative in structure.

Finally, we observe that novelists and philosophers hold several more things in common. Both experience and explore a common reality by participating in the various levels of reality that are made accessible to them by their composite human nature of body, intellect, imagination, soul, and spirit. Both rely upon metaphorical and analogical language to communicate their genuine experiences of a reality visible and invisible, material and immaterial, existent and nonexistent.[18] Both novelists and philosophers seek to express in their works the experiences of wonder and meaning that are vouchsafed them by reality.

This study began long ago when I was read (and later read myself) the stories of Noah's ark, Joseph's coat of many colors, and Daniel in the lion's den; and later those of Shakespeare and Dickens, of Pasternak and Dostoyevsky, of William Faulkner, Tillie Olsen, and Flannery O'Connor. While throughout my professional career—now approaching forty years—I have wondered and marveled at literature, the questions I have asked may now be distilled. How is the novel as a symbolic literary form equivalent to philosophy as the symbolic literary form understood and

17. Ibid., 174. Emphasis added.
18. See "Reality: nonexistent reality" in the glossary.

practiced by Eric Voegelin? What unites fiction and philosophy in the common quest to understand our nature, our world, and our cosmos?

From Aristotle we know that philosophy begins in wonder and that because "the myth is composed of wonders"[19] the *philomythos,* the lover of myth, is also a *philosophos,* a lover of wisdom. Wonder and the "awe of existence" not only underlie the human experience of meaning but also serve to initiate the philosophical search in those who are called to search, as was Eric Voegelin. If there exists a connection between myth and wonder, must there not also exist a connection between literature and wonder? Is the serious novelist not also a *philomythos* and a *philosophos?*

To explore and reflect upon these basic questions, I begin in part one, "The Philosopher," with Voegelin's principles of literary criticism—articulated primarily in his correspondence with the Shakespearean scholar Robert B. Heilman—in chapter 1. Chapter 2 discusses some central components of Voegelin's philosophy, especially those relevant to understanding the relation between philosophy and novels. In chapter 3, I examine the reader's relationship to a novel and its author. Part one, then, lays the foundations of Voegelin's literary criticism and philosophy as prelude to reading specific novels in chapters 4 through 6. In Part two, "The Storyteller," I interpret Graham Swift's *Waterland* in chapter 4, "The Barren Quest," as an agonized search for "when things went wrong." Chapter 5, "A Secret between Man and God," explores the deformation and recovery of reality in Heimito von Doderer's *The Demons.* Chapter 6, "Novel of Divine Presence," argues that Flannery O'Connor's *The Violent Bear It Away* envisions in the Time of the Tale, the flux of divine presence. Finally, the epilogue, "Our Love of Life, Children, Our Love of Life," meditates upon the reading of literature.

19. Aristotle *Metaphysics* 982b11–982b14, trans. Ross, p. 692.

# PART I

## THE
## PHILOSOPHER

# 1

## "One of My Permanent Occupations"

### Eric Voegelin as Literary Critic

The occupation with works of art, poetry, philosophy, mythical imagination and so forth, makes sense only if it is conducted as an inquiry into the nature of man.

~ Eric Voegelin to Robert B. Heilman

---

There are many reasons for writing a book that relies upon the philosophical work of Eric Voegelin for the interpretation of modern literature. Not the least of these is Voegelin's own understanding of the nature of his work and vocation. In a letter dated December 19, 1955, he wrote to his friend Robert B. Heilman, the English literature scholar and literary critic:

> Your letter of Dec. 11th came just in time this morning, for I wanted to write you today anyway to thank you for the delightful review of *Critics and Criticism*. It had thrown me into a mood of indecision, because your refined politeness left me in doubt whether I should not read the volume, because literary criticism is after all one of my permanent occupations. (*AFIL*, letter 57, p. 142)[1]

Eric Voegelin considered literary criticism one of his permanent occupations because of the necessity that confronted him as he

---

1. References to letters in the Heilman-Voegelin correspondence will be made by letter number, date, and page number within parentheses as they appear in *Robert B. Heilman and Eric Voegelin: A Friendship in Letters, 1944–1984,* ed. Embry (hereinafter referred to as *AFIL*). All letters in this chapter, unless otherwise noted, are taken from this correspondence. See appendix 1 for a brief overview of literary contents of this correspondence.

worked toward the preparation of what he intended as his first major work in English—*The History of Political Ideas.* In order to command his material, Voegelin began systematically working through the primary texts left by human beings who had themselves searched for, explored, and articulated the nature of their humanity and its order. Confronting these ancient documents led Voegelin to reflect upon how a modern scholar could understand these literary works by penetrating to the experiences that had engendered their articulations in stories, myths, scripture, dialogues, and treatises. While working on the *History of Political Ideas* in 1952, and still several years before his abandonment of that project and its replacement with *Order and History* (volume I was published in 1956), he wrote to his friend Heilman, asking him to read (and mark for correction any errors) the "MS of the first chapter of the *History of Political Ideas,* which [is] supposed to develop the principles of interpretation for the whole subsequent study. The chapter, thus, has a certain importance, both as the first one and as the statement of principles" (letter 37, May 3, 1952, p. 107). Indeed, this manuscript was to become the introduction to the heir of the abandoned *History of Political Ideas,* namely, *Order and History.* The reflections contained therein expanded beyond the development of interpretive principles that guided Voegelin's reading of texts into a philosophical search not only for manifestations of order in history but also for the ground of being and the destiny of humanity.

Voegelin's considered observations focusing specifically on literature, literary issues, and literary criticism, and the philosophical issues that flow from these—perhaps nowhere more explicitly expressed than in his correspondence with Heilman—appear in four places in that correspondence:

1. explicit principles of literary criticism expressed in letters 63 (July 24, 1956) and 65 (August 22, 1956) in response to his reading and responding to *Magic in the Web,* Heilman's book on *Othello;*
2. brief comments on interpretive method with specific statements on the use of language in imaginative works contained in letter 9 (April 9, 1946) as response to Heilman's *Lear* MS, later published as *This Great Stage;*
3. a substantive interpretation of Henry James's *The Turn of the Screw* found in letter 11 (November 13, 1947), supplemented by more explicit attention to the philosophical dimensions of literary

interpretation in his 1971 postscript to the earlier letter, both of
which are published in *Southern Review;*

4. a substantive sketch that focused on literature and myth found in
   letter 103 (August 13, 1964), which drew Heilman's attention to
   the symbol "Time of the Tale."

While an examination of the principles of Voegelin's criticism offers
an obvious starting point in looking at his work with literature, it must
be emphasized before we begin that his philosophy and philosophical
work provide the framework within which these principles are embedded. In fact, Heilman recognized this characteristic in Voegelin's work.
In his remembrance of Voegelin, first published in the winter 1996 issue
of *Southern Review,* Heilman, while identifying his own form of literary
criticism as "psychological" analysis, remarked that Voegelin found in
literature "an interplay of philosophical issues and spiritual forces, a
clash of symbols rather than a confrontation of psyches."[2]

For a literary critic to be first and foremost a philosopher would
appear to be a formidable qualification, but in returning to the Platonic
understanding of that term—as Voegelin did—we find that a philosopher need only be a lover of wisdom. This is a very important understanding of the term *philosopher,* because it places the accent on *lover*
without forcing a definition of *wisdom.* The philosophical search in
which a lover of wisdom engages is fundamentally Socratic, characterized by an essential humility and knowing ignorance, which requires
the philosopher to recognize that for human beings there can be no
final, complete knowledge of wisdom. A philosopher must remain open
to a continual search that builds, nonetheless, on the activities and
insights of all individuals so engaged. The philosophical search, however, proceeds from a foundational experiential knowledge, for as
Socrates says in his *Apology,* "to do wrong, and to disobey those who are
better than myself, whether god or man, that I know to be bad and dis-
graceful."[3] The philosopher then can discover and experience the
ground of being even though this ground remains rooted in mystery
and cognitively impenetrable. For Voegelin, as we will see, it is the
human lot to exist in the *metaxy,* the In-Between, and to participate in
reality with the "body, soul, intellect, and spirit."[4]

2. Reprinted in Heilman, *The Professor and the Profession,* 90.
3. Plato *Apology* 29B, in Plato, *Great Dialogues,* trans. Rouse, 435.
4. Voegelin, *New Science of Politics,* 91–92.

Since Voegelin's philosophy of consciousness occupies center stage in his work, the consciousness and modes of consciousness of the writer-creator, the reader, and the critic are crucial in any sort of Voegelinian literary criticism. Like the writer, the reader and the critic must rely on consciousness as the site in which the imaginative act of criticism occurs. But what is consciousness and what is the empirical ground upon which the critic's consciousness lays claim to the truth of his criticism? To begin to address this question, we must consider the hermeneutical principles of two critical letters that Voegelin wrote to Heilman in 1956.

## VOEGELIN'S PRINCIPLES OF LITERARY CRITICISM

In 1956, Heilman had published his study of *Othello, Magic in the Web,* and dedicated it to Voegelin. This dedication furnished the occasion for a remarkable exchange of ideas on literary criticism. In the same year, Voegelin had published *Israel and Revelation* (volume I of *Order and History*), the first book-length study to result from the abandoned *History of Political Ideas,* on which he had worked since 1939. Voegelin's approach to literary criticism is revealed in this exchange and is susceptible of reduction to three "simple," yet interwoven and dependent, principles.

### THE LITERARY CRITIC MUST EXHAUST THE SOURCE

This principle is easy enough to understand as rooted in a common-sense approach to literary texts. Of course one must first give precedence to the text itself. In order to exhaust the source, however, the critic must assume "the role of the disciple who has everything to learn from the master." The corollary to this assumption—that the critic must recognize that the author knew what he was doing when he wrote the text—is rooted not only in common sense but also in the basic humility with which a reader-critic must approach works of literature, especially the literary "classics" of antiquity. This first principle, along with its assumptions and elaborations, emerges in the context of Voegelin's letter dated July 24, 1956. He had written to Heilman in order to convey his gratitude for the dedication "in the only way I can thank, by response to the contents" (letter 63, p. 150). This response opens with the observation that the formal quality of the book—its construction, which requires the reader "to read it from the beginning in order to get its full

import"—"is intimately bound up with your method and your philosophical position." Voegelin then proceeded to identify "exhaustion of
the source" as the first principle of *Magic,* and to explain that this formal
principle was the fundamental attitude with which he approached classical literary texts himself, for "no adequate interpretation of a major
work is possible, unless the interpreter assumes the role of the disciple
who has everything to learn from the master" (ibid.). Exhaustion of the
source is grounded by several assumptions: (1) that the author "knew"
what he was doing; (2) that the parts of the text work together; and (3)
that the "texture of the linguistic corpus" gives rise to meaning (ibid.).

### THE LITERARY CRITIC MUST RELY UPON AN INTERPRETIVE TERMINOLOGY THAT IS CONSISTENT WITH THE LANGUAGE SYMBOLS OF THE SOURCE ITSELF

This second principle grows from the first. The critic who submits
to the master as a disciple must discipline himself if he is to understand
the words of the master. This discipline imposes upon such a critic an
interpretive terminology consistent with the language symbols of the
source and will ensure, as far as possible, that an interpretive scheme
that is external to the source itself will obscure neither the meanings
embedded in the text nor the intentions of its author. The critic, extending the interpretation as far as the symbols will allow, thus fulfills the
primary directive to "exhaust the source." Voegelin argued that exhaustion of the source requires that "the terminology of the interpretation,
if not identical with the language symbols of the source (a condition
that can frequently be fulfilled in the case of first-rate philosophers, but
rarely in the case of a poem or a myth), must not be introduced from
the 'outside', but be developed in closest contact with the source itself
for the purpose of differentiating the meanings which are apparent in
the work" (letter 63, p. 151). By rigorously following this second principle, the critic will avoid imposing an interpretation on the work that the
work itself will not sustain.

### THE CRITIC MUST DEVELOP A "SYSTEM" OF INTERPRETATION THAT EXTENDS THE POET'S COMPACT SYMBOLIZATIONS IN THE SAME DIRECTION INDICATED BY THE POET INTO A *PHILOSOPHICALLY CRITICAL LANGUAGE*

At this point, Voegelin maintained that the work of the literary
critic is simply an analytical, rational continuation of an author's work

along the tracks laid out in the work of art itself. The discipline, in Heilman's case, of rigorously adhering to the language of the play (*Othello*) extended from a "strand of compact motifs to the more immediate differentiations and distinctions in terms of a phenomenology of morals" (letter 63, p. 151). Because of the compactness of the symbolic language of the work, the literary critic can only rely upon the "linguistic corpus" until he has exhausted the meanings embedded therein. At that point, the critic must develop a "system" of interpretation that extends the poet's compact symbolizations in the same direction indicated by the poet into a philosophically critical language. After exhausting the source by following the author's symbols as far as they can be extended in interpretation, the critic must now translate the analytical immediacy of the poet's compact symbolism "of the whole of human nature that in the poem is carried by the magic in the web," into the rational order of his work in which the "whole of human nature" must "now be carried by the magic of the system." "And here," Voegelin praised Heilman for his work, "I am now full of admiration for your qualities as a philosopher. For you have arranged the problem of human nature in the technically perfect order of progress from the peripheral to the center of personality. . . . You begin with . . . the problem of appearance and reality; and you end with the categories of existence and spiritual order—with life and death, love and hate, eros and caritas, transfiguration and demonic silence" (letter 63, p. 152).

This final principle of literary criticism goes to the heart of the human understanding of reality and to the heart of the philosophical enterprise. Here, in 1956, Voegelin is beginning to articulate his discovery of the importance of a critical-analytical consciousness—a consciousness that is especially important in cases where the artist creates works that symbolize deformations of human consciousness and, accordingly, the structure of reality.[5] The principles of Voegelin's literary criticism thus were articulated within a larger framework; and whenever he discoursed on literary issues in his letters to Heilman, he placed these issues within a philosophical-historical context. While in letter 57 (December 19, 1955), Voegelin had commented almost offhandedly that literary criticism was one of his "permanent occupations," we learn in letter 65 (August 22, 1956) that literary criticism "makes sense only if it is conducted as an inquiry into the nature of man" (letter 65, p. 157).

---

5. See below for a fuller development of this critical-analytical consciousness as crucial to the literary critic.

To inquire into the nature of man involves the literary critic in historical inquiry, and it is clear that Voegelin understands Heilman's literary criticism in this context, since he consistently refers to him as a
historian of literature rather than as a literary critic. Responding to
Heilman's comments in a letter of August 19, 1956, which focused on
the historical relativism characteristic of the academic debates within
the narrower discipline of literary criticism itself,[6] Voegelin articulated
his position that human existence is historical existence, that human
nature is revealed in the historical documents (literature) of the past,
and that the revelation of human nature in the literature of the past is
thus the basis for his literary criticism. "Your letter," Voegelin writes,

> supplies at least some of the items that were beyond my diagnostic abil-
> ities—and I can summarize them now as the historism apparently ram-
> pant in literary criticism.
>      . . . The various questions which you indicate in your letter seem to me
> to be all connected with the effort to find the critical basis beyond histor-
> ical relativism, and by that token they are connected with each other. The
> question of the "was" and the "is" that you raise is, for instance, in my
> opinion only another facet of the question raised earlier in your letter
> that, on the one hand, one can only get out of the play what one brings to
> it while, on the other hand, if one lays oneself open to the play, one can
> get considerably more out of it than one thought one had brought to it.
> Let me dwell a bit on this issue, because it is after all the central issue of
> my life as a scholar and apparently yours, too. (letter 65, p. 156)

Dwelling upon the problem of historicism, Voegelin argued that to
understand the revelation of human nature in various literary forms is

6. See letter 64 in *AFIL*, where Heilman writes: "I was driven [to distinguish two
aspects of a work—the 'was' and the 'is'] by the dominance of historical studies, in
which it is assumed that the work has a single reality which is derivable only from the
historical context. This seems dangerous nonsense to me (and I need not explain to you
that I do not contemn historical studies), for it appears to deny the existence of a non-
historical permanence which I find inseparable from myth, fable, the artistic formula-
tions of the imagination, etc. Maybe 'is' is too tricky a metaphor for this; I'm not sure.
The second point followed from this: my assumption of the power of the critic to view
the work, at least in part, non-historically, i.e., to transcend the intellectual and cultural
climate of his own time and thus to be able to identify in the work those elements that
conform to the eternal truth of things. The historical relativists argue, of course, not
only that the work is relative only to its times, but that the mind of the critic is relative
only to his own times, in which he is hopelessly enclosed. Therefore the practice of literary history is the only true humility in the literary student; the critic who pretends to
be doing anything but historicizing is an egomaniac. So I postulate his share in the
divine power to see all times [in] simultaneity" (letter 64, August 19, 1956, p. 155).

the raison d'être of literary criticism itself. In the same letter, Voegelin asserts:

> The occupation with works of art, poetry, philosophy, mythical imagina-
> tion, and so forth, makes sense only if it is conducted as an inquiry into the
> nature of man. That sentence, while it excludes historicism, does not
> exclude history, for it is peculiar to the nature of man that it unfolds its
> potentialities historically. Not that historically anything "new" comes up—
> human nature is always wholly present—but there are modes of clarity
> and degrees of comprehensiveness in man's understanding of his self and
> his position in the world. . . . Hence, the study of the classics is the princi-
> pal instrument of self-education; and if one studies them with loving care,
> as you most truly observe, one all of a sudden discovers that one's under-
> standing of a great work increases (and also one's ability to communicate
> such understanding) for the good reason that the student has increased
> through the process of study—and that after all is the purpose of the enter-
> prise. (At least it is my purpose in spending the time of my life in the study
> of prophets, philosophers, and saints.) . . . History is the unfolding of the
> human Psyche; historiography is the reconstruction of the unfolding
> through the psyche of the historian. The basis of historical interpretation
> is the identity of substance (the psyche) in the object and the subject of
> interpretation; and its purpose is participation in the great dialogue that
> goes through the centuries among men about their nature and destiny.
> And participation is impossible without growth in stature (within the per-
> sonal limitations) toward the rank of the best; and that growth is impossi-
> ble unless one recognizes authority and surrenders to it. (ibid., p. 157)

Since the human psyche unfolds in history, the primary work of the historian is to reconstruct, imaginatively (as we shall argue below), this
unfolding. That the historian *can* reconstruct the historical unfolding of
the psyche is dependent upon the reality that the substance of the
human psyche is shared by both the object of the interpretation (the
writer, or rather the human being who articulated and symbolized his
experiences in language) and the subject of the interpretation (the historian of literature/literary critic). The shared spiritual substance of the
writer and the historian/critic makes possible the participation of the
historian (as well as all future historians) in "the great dialogue that
goes through the centuries among men about their nature and destiny."
Participation in the great dialogue makes personal spiritual growth possible, but "growth is impossible" unless the historian/critic "recognizes
authority and surrenders to it" (letter 65, p. 157). Thus we return full
circle to Voegelin's first principle of literary criticism—"exhaustion of

the source"—and its corollary, the critic's assumption of the "role of the disciple who has everything to learn from the master" (letter 63, p. 150).

## Language and Symbol in Voegelin's Literary Criticism

Even before the important exchange of 1956, Voegelin had responded to Heilman's *King Lear* manuscript, later published as *This Great Stage: Image and Structure in* King Lear, with remarks on the relationship between the language of the source and the attention the critic must pay to the linguistic symbols in the source itself. Here he commented on the method necessary for analyzing the pattern of imagery in an imaginative poetic work like *Lear*. He remarked that

> not all of the language-body of the drama has significance as symbolism for the transcendent meaning. A word like "see" may have symbolic function in the structure of the whole, or it may be irrelevant to it because its meaning is confined to a limited pragmatic context—as when a person would say "Look here" or "There you see" in a determinative, pragmatic sense, without implications concerning the metaphysical problem of "insight." Here begins the art of the interpreter who has to catch all the "sees" which have a function as transcendent symbols and to omit the "sees" that have no such function. (letter 9, April 9, 1946, pp. 31–32)

Insofar as the medium of language conveys meaning that transcends the level of sensual symbolism, Voegelin indicated that

> the sight-pattern that runs through the *King Lear* can be a basic symbolic structure for the higher levels of meaning because the world of the senses is loaded, indeed, with meanings beyond the physical context. . . . "[E]yes" are not just optical apparatuses but mediums of intelligence. *Here, as far as I can see, lies the root of the symbolic value which words denoting sensual objects and functions can gain in the context of a poem. The word-body of a verse can be loaded with meanings beyond the meaning explicitly contained in the sentence as a grammatical unit. That is to say: in a poem (and for that matter also in good prose; with certain limits) the implied meaning of the word-body can be used to echo, amplify, surround with fringes, etc., the explicit meaning of the statements. This raises the second methodological question: the question of the interlocking of word-symbols as carriers of implied meanings, with the explicit meanings of the text.* (letter 9, pp. 32–33; emphasis added)

Voegelin was raising an issue here that he would focus on later in another context: the importance of understanding that language, while employed in its pragmatic function for communicating about the objective world of things, may also be used symbolically in imaginative ways to transcend objective reality, thereby expressing meaning that transcends the objective world to symbolize a nonobjective or nonexistent reality. Nonexistent reality—nonexistent in the sense that it is eternal Being that suffuses the world of becoming (and of ceasing) things in time—must be communicated analogically and symbolically through the only means available to human beings, the language of things.[7] In any particular piece of imaginative writing, the interpreter must then distinguish in the language of the work between the pragmatic uses of the linguistic terms signifying things and the occasions on which those words are used to suggest the meaning inherent in the experiences that the creator-writer is exploring through imaginative symbolization.

## VOEGELIN'S CRITICISM OF HENRY JAMES'S *THE TURN OF THE SCREW*

A third significant statement regarding literary criticism originated in the Heilman-Voegelin correspondence and culminated with the publication in 1971 of a postscript to a letter first written by Voegelin in 1947. Voegelin's analysis focused on *The Turn of the Screw* by Henry James as a response to a critique that Heilman had published of a Freudian interpretation of the novella.[8] In his postscript, Voegelin raised the twin issues of the "dustiness" of the symbols in James's story and the consequent necessity that a valid literary criticism must be firmly based upon a critical-existential assessment by the critic. These issues led to a conversation between Donald E. Stanford, editor of the *Southern Review,* and Voegelin.

After Stanford completed work on the issue in which both Voegelin's original letter on James's *The Turn of the Screw* and the newly written

7. Cf. Voegelin, *In Search of Order,* 42.
8. Heilman, "The Freudian Reading of *The Turn of the Screw.*" Voegelin's 1947 letter to Heilman was published in a lead article, entitled "*The Turn of the Screw,*" in the *Southern Review,* n.s. 7 (1971): 9–48. In addition to Voegelin's original letter, this lead article contained Donald E. Stanford, "A Prefatory Note"; Heilman, "Foreword"; Voegelin, "A Letter to Robert B. Heilman"; and Voegelin, "Postscript: On Paradise and Revolution."

postscript appeared, Stanford and his wife visited the Voegelins at their home in Palo Alto. The Stanfords' visit in the summer of 1970 was followed by an exchange of letters that continued the conversation, in the course of which they had discussed poetry and poetic quality. Stanford had mentioned a poem, "The Course of a Particular," by Wallace Stevens (used in Stanford's "Prefatory Note"). After the get-together in Palo Alto, Stanford wrote Voegelin (August 27), enclosing a copy of that poem and another by Stevens. Voegelin responded, recalling "the splendid evening of our discussion here in Stanford":

> On that occasion you stressed very strongly that the formal quality of a work of art is the one and only quality a literary critic has to take into account. And, if I remember correctly, I expressed equally strongly *the opinion that in a critical judgment there must also be taken into account the existential content.* On that evening, our argument referred to the work of Henry James and some opinion I had expressed about its "dustiness" in my paper. Now I have similar hesitations about Stevens' poem.[9]

Voegelin's view that "critical judgment" must take into account "the existential content" of a literary work, in this case a poem, represents an advance on the third principle of literary criticism identified above, namely, the importance of a critical-analytical consciousness for the literary critic that permits him to evaluate and judge the quality of a literary work. Although this critical awareness is formulated as "reflective distance" in his late work, in the "Postscript" (finished in December 1969) Voegelin was already formulating a symbol for denoting this awareness.[10] "Reflective distance" is articulated in the posthumous last volume of *Order and History* as part of the complex "Reflective Distance-Remembrance-Oblivion" discovered in the philosopher's meditation—e.g., Plato's and Voegelin's. In this late work, "reflective distance" appears to be equivalent to what Voegelin designates as "critical distance" and the "critical-analytical consciousness" of the literary critic in the "Postscript." "Critical distance," of course, applies also to the literary artist and his awareness (1) that he is creating a work of art and (2) that he is aware of what he has experienced and is symbolizing in his work.

The term *critical distance* developed as Voegelin increasingly recognized the deformation of consciousness that informs much modern

---

9. Voegelin Papers, Hoover Institute, box 36, folder 34. Emphasis added.
10. Cf. especially *In Search of Order,* 54–56, 58–59. See also Voegelin, "Postscript: On Paradise and Revolution," *Southern Review,* 27, 39–40.

thought and literature. He came to understand deformed consciousness as closure to or revolt against reality as it had been experienced and symbolized in myth and philosophy. Ancient mytho-poets and philosophers symbolized the quaternarian structure of reality (i.e., the community of being: God, man, world, and society), and Voegelin recognized that significant segments of modernity were locked in closure to reality structured in this way. This closure marked for Voegelin the deformation of consciousness that he only sensed as he wrote the earlier letter to Heilman but explicitly identified as the "dustiness" of the Jamesian symbols as he was writing the postscript for the *Southern Review*. In the "Postscript," he elaborated:

> The deformation of which I am speaking is the fateful shift in Western society from existence in openness toward the cosmos to existence in the mode of closure against, and denial of, its reality. As the process gains momentum, the symbols of open existence—God, man, the divine origin of the cosmos, and the divine Logos permeating its order—lose the vitality of their truth and are eclipsed by the imagery of a self-creative, self-realizing, self-expressing, self-ordering, and self-saving ego that is thrown into, and confronted with, an immanently closed world.[11]

On the "dustiness" of James's garden (in the story) and its deformed humanity, Voegelin asserts that the work's existential defect "reflects a warping in the author's consciousness of reality, while the mode of closure in the author's existence translates itself into a want of critical distance in the work. . . . Even in an extreme case, however, the critical distance cannot be abolished [al]together; for if there were no distance at all, there would be no work of art but only a man's syndrome of his pathological state."[12] Since works of this type are difficult to understand, it is left to the reader to "supply the critical consciousness of reality" and to discern in what manner reality is deformed, for in such a case he "cannot simply follow the symbolism wherever it leads and expect to come out with something that makes sense in terms of reality."[13] Furthermore, the reader must beware of using as an instrument of interpretation one or the other of the prevailing theories of

---

11. Voegelin, "Postscript: On Paradise and Revolution," in *Published Essays, 1966–1985,* 151. Further citations of "Postscript" will be to this version.

12. Ibid., 162–63. Cf. Voegelin, "Wisdom and the Magic of the Extreme," 315–75, and Voegelin, *The Ecumenic Age,* 291–303.

13. Voegelin, "Postscript," 152.

interpretation, such as the psychoanalytic theories, since they are themselves "symbolizations of deformed existence" that participate in the modern proclivity for closure to reality, i.e., to the whole community of being.[14] This discussion, aimed by Voegelin at the problems arising out of interpreting *The Turn of the Screw,* also provides a further clue to the approach that a literary critic must take when confronted with a work of art where the artist has not arrived at the "critical distance" necessary for adequately symbolizing human experience in openness to reality. A philosophy of existence that remains open to the community of being and the ground of Being is necessary for the literary critic who desires to understand works of literature and their place in the trail of symbols left by the human search for order.[15]

Commenting that his earlier, and to some extent failed, attempt in the original letter to arrive at a "full understanding of the *nouvelle*" by directly tracing the symbols themselves, Voegelin nevertheless argued that he had met the first demand on the critic "inasmuch as they [the symbols] correctly identify major parts of the reality deformed: God, man, the soul, the drama of salvation and damnation." The earlier attempt at interpretation could, however, be used to meet the second task "of ascertaining the nature of the deformation." In fulfillment of this second task, Voegelin examined the androgynic myth as adopted from ancient mythology and then deformed for the building of modern Edens such as James's garden in *The Turn of the Screw.* Voegelin distinguished between ancient symbols and the modern "symbols which derive their meaning from the mode of closure they express":

> The ancient mythopoets were critically conscious of the non-Edenic character of reality. When they developed speculative symbols within the medium of the myth, they knew they were symbolizing *le mystère de la totalité* in a cosmos whose order was marred by strife, injustice, unreason, and death. Moreover, they were not spiritual illiterates who would transform a symbol engendered by an experience of imperfection into a program of perfection in this world. . . . This degradation or perversion is the common denominator in the modern symbolist use of symbols, in the same sense as the experience of non-Edenic reality is the common denominator of ancient mythopoesy.[16]

14. Ibid.
15. This book itself is rooted in the conviction that Voegelin's philosophy will provide the literary critic the necessary philosophical "tools" for understanding the call of stories and the human condition as it is explored in works of literature.
16. Ibid., 152, 153, 170–71.

## LITERATURE AND THE TIME OF THE TALE

From general interpretive attitudes and principles, we turn now to one of Voegelin's substantive statements about literature. This statement, which I quote *in toto,* will in turn lead us into the heart, and the complexity, of his philosophical work. On August 13, 1964, Voegelin wrote to Heilman from Munich:

> There was a point in my Salzburg lecture that might interest you as an historian of literature: The basic form of myth, the "tale" in the widest sense, including the epic as well as the dramatic account of happenings, has a specific time, immanent to the tale, whose specific character consists in the ability to combine human, cosmic and divine elements into one story. I have called it, already in *Order and History,* the Time of the Tale. It expresses the experience of being (that embraces all sorts of reality, the cosmos) in flux. This Tale with its Time seems to me the primary literary form, peculiar to cosmological civilizations. Primary in the sense that it precedes all literary form developed under conditions of differentiating experiences: If man becomes differentiated with any degree of autonomy from the cosmic context, then, and only then, will develop specifically human forms of literature: The story of human events, lyric, empirical history, the drama and tragedy of human action, the meditative dialogue in the Platonic sense, etc. Underlying all later, differentiated forms, however, there remains the basic Tale which expresses Being in flux. Time, then, would not be an empty container into which you can fill any content, but there would be as many times as there are types of differentiated content. Think for instance of Proust's *temps perdu* and *temps retrouvé* as times which correspond to the loss and rediscovery of self, the action of rediscovery through a monumental literary work of remembrance being the atonement for the loss of time through personal guilt—very similar to cosmological rituals of restoring order that has been lost through lapse of time. I believe the regrets of Richard II (I wasted time and now does time waste me) touch the same problem. This reflexion would lead into a philosophy of language, in which the basic Tale would appear as the instrument of man's dealing with reality through language—and adequately at that. Form and content, thus, would be inseparable: The Tale, if it is any good, has to deal with Being in flux, however much differentiated the insights into the complex structures of reality may be.[17] (letter 103, p. 223)

17. In an August 31, 1958, letter to Heilman, Voegelin wrote that "at present I am struggling with the literary form of the Gospels which, as always, is inseparable from its content—but at least some notable results are in sight now. When I have finished this section, I shall be greatly relieved, for the Gospels are, after all, a cornerstone in the

Voegelin's specific references to Proust's *A la recherche du temps perdu* and to Shakespeare's *Richard II* suggest that the symbolic formulation "Time of the Tale" is a critical tool for approaching and interpreting literature in general, modern literature in particular, and, even more specifically, modern novels. The Time of the Tale also informs Voegelin's late work and reveals ways in which the insights of his late meditations are prefigured in his earlier work. Moreover, understanding the Time of the Tale and the philosophical context from which it emerged in Voegelin's work permits us to see and read modern novels as crucial parts of a historical philosophical enterprise that are built upon more than the idiosyncratic expressions of the private dream worlds of Heraclitus's sleepwalkers and their counterparts among modern novelists. Indeed, perhaps specific works of modern literature—read in the context of the Time of the Tale and Voegelin's work generally—will gain the stature of an Aeschylus's *Oresteia*, in which "to those who are awake, there is one ordered universe common (to all)."[18]

The passage from letter 103 opens up a truly panoramic perspective on Voegelin's late-mature work and also indicates how the early work, especially in the first three volumes of *Order and History*, prefigures his later work—*Anamnesis* (1966), *The Ecumenic Age* (1974), and the posthumous *In Search of Order* (1987). Letter 103 (from 1964) is not the first place Voegelin used the symbol "Time of the Tale," however. We also find the phrase in *Israel and Revelation* (1956) and *Plato and Aristotle* (1957), as well as in three works after the 1964 letter: the essay "Was ist Natur?"(1965), *The Ecumenic Age* (1974), and "The Beginning and the Beyond: *A Meditation on Truth*" (1977). Voegelin continued to explore in his late work the complexes of reality that underlie the Time of the Tale. For example, in *In Search of Order*, Voegelin meditates on myth and mytho-speculation, on the Beginning, and on Plato's *Timaeus*, a work that figured prominently in the first use of the Time of the Tale in *Plato and Aristotle*. The contexts in which all the uses of the term appear reflect topics that we can identify from the paragraph in letter 103:

---

spiritual history of the West" (*AFIL*, letter 79, p. 183). In this letter, Voegelin is already struggling with the central component of the Time of the Tale, namely, Being in flux or, alternatively, the flux of divine presence. And since the Gospels contain the story of the Incarnation—the timelessness of divine presence revealing Itself in time—I think that he already sensed that he was dealing with the Time of the Tale, in which form merged with content. In the Christian universe of discourse, insofar as I know, he only dealt with the Time of the Tale in one place and that was in his discussion of Saint Paul in *The Ecumenic Age*. Clearly the Gospels merge form and content in their Tale.

18. Fragments from *Ancilla*, trans. Freeman.

1. myth as the primary literary form of cosmological civilizations[19]
2. differentiation of insights into the structures of reality and subsequent literary forms as a historical event
3. the relation between myth, Time of the Tale, and other literary forms
4. the Time of the Tale in relation to other types of time
5. the Time of the Tale and Being in flux
6. the persistence of the Time of the Tale after differentiation of insights into other complex structures of reality
7. the merger of form and content in the basic Tale
8. a philosophy of language

These topics in turn lead one to other cognate, intimately interrelated topics—especially the primary experience of the cosmos, styles of truth, types of myth, historiogenesis, equivalences of symbolic expressions, the Beginning and the ground of Being, the truth of the myth, observations on language and imagination, and interrelationships between myth and the other symbolic forms of philosophy and revelation.

It becomes obvious that the Time of the Tale is integrally bound up with myths, that is, works of art that symbolize the experiences of human beings in cosmological civilizations. In "In Search of the Ground" (1965), Voegelin replied, in response to a question about the identification of a ground in relation to aesthetic concerns, that "all art, if it is any good, is some sort of a myth in the sense that it becomes what I call a *cosmion*, a reflection of the unity of the cosmos as a whole. . . . It's much closer to cosmological thinking than anything else."[20] About three years later, in "Anxiety and Reason" (finished c. 1968), Voegelin writes that "the myth has not remained a mere object of inquiry but has become an active force in the creation of new symbols expressing the human condition. The new situation will be suggested if there be named

19. The reader who would like better to understand Voegelin's use of the term *cosmological civilization* and its literary symbolization, "myth," should begin by consulting Voegelin's *Israel and Revelation* (vol. I of *Order and History*), *The Ecumenic Age* (vol. IV of *Order and History*), and perhaps the Candler Lectures, "The Drama of Humanity," in vol. 33 of *The Collected Works of Eric Voegelin*. In his late work, Voegelin came to understand that the myth is never supplanted by the differentiations of revelation and philosophy but must, rather, symbolically ground the later differentiations, just as the primary experience of the cosmos—participation in the primordial community of being—must suffuse and invigorate the cognitive-linguistic-imaginative participation of consciousness in the cognitive-meditative-imaginative structure of reality.

20. Voegelin, "In Search of the Ground," 240.

representatively the work of James Joyce, William Butler Yeats, and Thomas Mann. In relation to the perversions both of transcendence and immanence, the revival must be acknowledged as a ritual restoration of order. The truth of the cosmos full of gods reasserts itself."[21]

For Voegelin it is clear that literature—in terms of both its experiential origins as well as its imaginative symbolization—is generically related to myth. That Voegelin understood a work of art as a cosmion reflecting the "unity of the cosmos as a whole" clearly connects it with a cosmological style of truth and myth that are both rooted in compact experiences of reality—the primary cosmic experience. Voegelin understood Time of the Tale to be the primary literary form in two senses: primary as prior to other literary forms and primary as foundational to and underlying all later literary forms that result from human understanding of differentiated reality. Literature, at least as we know it in the modern era, is created in a time after the differentiation of reality into immanence and transcendence.[22] However, only when the tale being told combines human, cosmic, and divine elements does it approach the status of myth or the Tale with its Time that is out of time. The Time of the Tale may indeed be an important critical aid for our understanding of the human experience as it has been articulated and symbolized by modern novels. Therefore, it behooves us at this point to focus for a bit on the related components of Voegelin's philosophical work. Before turning to this discussion of Voegelin's philosophy, however, several further observations about his understanding of literary criticism are in order.

## Voegelin's Literary Criticism: An Overview

First, when Voegelin uses the term *literary criticism*, he applies it to literature both narrowly and broadly defined. On the one hand, *literary criticism* may mean the principles used in the interpretation of literature that falls into the modern disciplinary divisions of knowledge such as "English literature," "the history of literature," or "Shakespeare

21. Voegelin, "Anxiety and Reason," 84.

22. There are certainly writers from traditions in which differentiation has not "occurred," or rather has occurred only externally to the tradition as an alien force, who have adopted the western, European novel form. This issue certainly would raise a number of interesting questions for exploration. For example, Hoye's work on Japanese novelists yields interesting observations about the "place" that literature (and hence the modern novel) occupies in Japanese society and culture. See Hoye, "Imagining Modern Japan: Natsume Soseki's First Trilogy."

studies." On the other hand, *literary criticism* may refer to the hermeneutical principles for interpreting literature that is understood to include any written document that articulates or expresses human experience symbolically and that relies upon the imaginative capacities of individual human beings to create and understand. Material that may be recognized as "literature" in this second sense thus may include not only modern novels, plays, and poems, but also epic poems, ancient tragedies and dramas, the Gospels, and even analyses of language such as those of Karl Kraus or George Orwell. Early in his correspondence with Heilman, especially in letter 9, April 9, 1946 (a commentary on Heilman's *Lear* manuscript), and letter 11, November 13, 1947 (the now famous commentary on *The Turn of the Screw*), he expresses a reticence to interlope into the specialized areas of Shakespeare or James studies. On April 9, 1946, Voegelin wrote, "You will not expect a dilettante to indulge in a critical evaluation of details. Only to prove the carefulness of my reading let me relate some of the notes which I penciled down while going through the MS" (letter 9, p. 31). Later, on December 30, 1969, Voegelin wrote a response to Heilman's comments on the *Turn* Postscript: "I am greatly relieved that you have no major objection to what I did with the Postscript. It seems that what you did when you initiated me to Henry James has come to a happy end after all. Of course, that is still not the last word about James by far, but I am quite content if you say that my effort is at least ahead of the current treatment of James in the expert literature" (letter 123, p. 258). On other occasions, Voegelin freely and without concern for such disciplinary boundaries drew into his philosophical work the symbols created by artists. Examples abound. From Heimito von Doderer's novel, *Die Dämonen*, he adopted the symbol "second reality,"[23] and from Flaubert he adopted "the *grotesque*" to replace "the *burlesque*" (that he had taken from his study of "novels and dramas by Doderer, Frisch and Dürrenmatt"), as a symbol for adequately representing an ideological distortion of reality of Gnostic symbolism (letter 107, February 22, 1965, p. 233). From Munich in August 1958, Voegelin wrote Heilman that "at present I am struggling with the literary form of the Gospels which, as always, is inseparable from its content—but at least some notable results are in sight now" (letter 79, August 31, 1958, p. 183). It is important to emphasize,

23. Voegelin, "Autobiographical Statement at Age Eighty-Two," 434. Elsewhere, Voegelin attributes the first use of *second reality* to the novelist Robert von Musil in *Der Mann ohne Eigenschaften* (*The Man without Qualities*).

then, that Voegelin's principles of literary criticism are equally applicable to both the narrow and broad definitions of literature.

Second, the principles of Voegelin's literary criticism are rooted in a commonsensical approach to the texts of the human spirit and to experiences of reality that these texts symbolize. As Voegelin himself expressed it to Ellis Sandoz: "the men who have the experiences express themselves through symbols; and the symbols are the key to understanding the experience expressed."[24] While this common-sense approach to literary texts is rooted in Voegelin's respect for the text and the author who wrote the text, as well as in a scholar's humility and refusal to privilege his own existence as a "modern" man, in a more technical way this common sense also undergirds much of his own approach to philosophy, especially after his discovery of English and American common sense philosophy.[25] Moreover, as Voegelin argues in letter 65, it would be impossible to understand historical texts if the contemporary critic did not share his own human nature with that of the creators of historical symbolizations.

Third, several crucial statements in Voegelin's work provide the empirical-theoretical attitude that philosophically grounds his literary criticism. He opens the preface to *Israel and Revelation*, volume I of *Order and History*, with the statement that "the order of history emerges from the history of order," thereby establishing the empirical-historical intention of his work.[26] In another startlingly bold declarative sentence, which opened the introduction to the same volume, Voegelin writes: "God and man, world and society form a primordial community of being." With this statement Voegelin announces both an empirical conclusion based upon his vast studies for the History of Political Ideas project and the range of an inquiry that would occupy his energies throughout the remainder of his life. After this opening, he continued: "The community with its quaternarian structure is, and is not, a datum of human experience. It is a datum of experience insofar as it is known to man by virtue of his participation in the mystery of its being. It is not

24. Quoted from *Autobiographical Memoir*, 81, in *The Voegelinian Revolution*, by Sandoz, 22.

25. See Voegelin, *Autobiographical Reflections*, 28–29. Common sense for Voegelin is a form of rationality, to include practicality, that has not been developed to a level of self-reflective philosophical proficiency. See Voegelin, *On the Form of the American Mind*, 29–31.

26. This sentence opened the manuscript that Voegelin asked Heilman to read in 1952, and it was retained as the opening sentence of the introduction when *Israel and Revelation* was published in 1956. Voegelin, *Israel and Revelation*, 19.

a datum of experience insofar as it is not given in the manner of an object of the external world but is knowable only from the perspective of participation in it."[27] It should be noted that by the time Voegelin writes the 1956 letters that are discussed above, he has already established the fundamental principles of his philosophy: that human existence is historical existence, that the reality to be understood through history is the community of being, that human existence is to be understood in the context of the community of being, and that human experience of that reality can only be known from the perspective of human participation in the community of being. These emphases focus attention upon the exploration of human nature and thus human consciousness; and art—to include literature—is seen by Voegelin as a vital resource for the philosopher who would understand human consciousness as it manifests itself historically in the biographies of concrete human beings through their imaginative symbolizations.

For Voegelin, then, "literature" supplies evidence that empirically grounds his inquiry into the historical existence of human beings as partners in the community of being. But literature and thus literary criticism occupy an even more personal place in the constellation of Voegelin's thought. Here it becomes rather difficult to delineate between Voegelin's philosophical enterprise and the personal quest that lies at its heart. It is in the person Eric Voegelin that vocation and philosophical inquiry intersect and come to be understood as rooted in the Platonic articulation of philosophy as the love of wisdom.[28] In an August 1956 letter, Voegelin wrote to Heilman that "the study of the classics is the principal instrument of self-education; and if one studies them with loving care, as you most truly observe, one all of a sudden discovers that one's understanding of a great work increases (and also one's ability to communicate such understanding) for the good reason that the student has increased through the process of study—and that after all is the purpose of the enterprise. (At least it is my purpose in spending the time of my life in the study of prophets, philosophers, and saints)" (letter 65, August 22, 1956, p. 157). Let me repeat and emphasize several phrases in this remarkable confession to Heilman. Note that, for Voegelin, "self-education" occurs through "the study of the classics." Against the backdrop of Voegelin's experience in Vienna during

27. Ibid., 39

28. The philosopher's consciousness, like that of any other human being, is historically formed and thus rooted in the biography of the philosopher. For the complete development of this insight see Voegelin, *Anamnesis*.

his early years, an experience that witnessed the breakdown of institutions and linguistic integrity, this self-education process takes on a heightened significance, for when the literary culture and the educational institutions upon which literacy depends are compromised and even destroyed, a man must look to the classics as guides to the recovery of his own humanity, to the recovery of his own integrity as a human being.

Self-education, however, can only occur if one approaches the classics with a reverent attitude of "loving care." This approach results in a sudden discovery: "that one's understanding of a great work increases (and also one's ability to communicate such understanding) for the good reason that the student has increased through the process of study." The result—an increase in spiritual stature—furthers the purpose for which one engaged in the study initially. And then Voegelin, even though he buries it in parentheses, makes a remarkable confession that articulates his vocation: "(At least it is my purpose in spending the time of my life in the study of prophets, philosophers, and saints)."

Finally, we must note that in this final confessional statement art, the arts, and thus literature, are absent from the final list of sources—the prophets, philosophers, and saints—that Voegelin spends the time of his life studying. Why? The quick response is that philosophy itself, as a symbolic form developed by Plato, relies upon and combines the literary forms of dialogue, myth, analysis, and anamnetic meditation to articulate experiences of the philosopher. Since it is now apparent that literary criticism in a Voegelinian mode is bound up with the philosophy that he developed over a lifetime of reading, research, reflection, and meditation, we now turn to a necessarily condensed exposition of his work—a consideration of Eric Voegelin's lifetime Search of Order.[29]

---

29. For those interested in exploring more thorough and detailed discussions and analyses of Voegelin's work, I suggest: Hughes, *Mystery and Myth in the Philosophy of Eric Voegelin;* essays by Jürgen Gebhardt and Frederick G. Lawrence in *International and Interdisciplinary Perspectives on Eric Voegelin,* ed. McKnight and Price; essays by Lewis P. Simpson, Paul Grimley Kuntz, and Paul Caringella in *Eric Voegelin's Significance for the Modern Mind,* ed. Sandoz; and, Sandoz, *The Voegelinian Revolution.*

# 2

# "The Attunement of the Soul"

## Eric Voegelin's Search of Order

On the coming of evening, I return to my house and enter my study; and . . . I enter the ancient courts of ancient men, where, received by them with affection, I feed on that food which only is mine and which I was born for, where I am not ashamed to speak with them and to ask them the reason for their actions; and they in their kindness answer me . . . I am not frightened by death; entirely I give myself over to them.

~ Niccolò Machiavelli to Francesco Vettori
*December 10, 1513*

At the time of his death, Voegelin left unfinished the fifth volume of *Order and History, In Search of Order,* which was published posthumously in 1987. Although the book is unfinished, its fragmentary nature should not "convey a suspicion of its being imperfectly deliberated," points out Ellis Sandoz in his introduction to the volume. For "it is fragmentary only in not extending the analysis to other materials plainly in the author's view and in not illustrating the theoretical presentation in greater detail than he was able to do before time ran out. But the theoretical presentation itself is essentially complete, and the fact that the quest of order is an unfinished story as told by Voegelin is most fitting."[1]

The various components of Voegelin's philosophy that I consider

1. Sandoz, Editor's Introduction to *In Search of Order,* 15.

crucial to a Voegelinian approach to literary works are not necessarily discussed in the order in which he wrote about or published them. This approach is justified by the fact that his thought, as we now see it whole, did not develop in a unilinear manner from an earlier position that must be discarded as new material is uncovered. Responding, late in his life, to the question of whether he would deny anything he had written in *Anamnesis* (1966), Voegelin replied, "No. I rarely have something to deny because I always stick close to the empirical materials and do not generalize beyond them. So when I generalize, I have to generalize because of the materials."[2] The historical materials that had been the foci of his early works continued to be the foci of his late meditations. Many examples could be adduced here, but a few prime examples would include Hesiod, the *Timaeus* of Plato, the *Metaphysics* of Aristotle, and the philosophy of Hegel. That he was unafraid to begin again at the beginning is evident in the title of the first chapter of *In Search of Order:* "The Beginning of the Beginning." Even a cursory examination of the book's Analytical Table of Contents by anyone familiar with the first four volumes of *Order and History* would reveal that Voegelin continually returned to materials he had already dealt with, deepening his insights and refining his linguistic expression as he probed the depths of his own soul in the manner first discovered by Heraclitus. The form that this chapter takes harkens back to and combines both strands—reflective meditation and historical recollection—of his empirical–experientially grounded philosophizing identified in 1966 as *anamnesis.*

## THE DOUBLE ORIGIN OF THE PHILOSOPHICAL QUEST: WONDER AND THE EXPERIENCE OF DISORDER

As Voegelin himself pointed out on many occasions, philosophy begins with the philosopher's personal experience of political and social disorder that arises from spiritual disorder. In Voegelin's case, the experience of disorder occurred in early twentieth-century Austria, especially the period between the two world wars, when he was personally in danger following the Anschluss. Philosophy also has a second empirical root: the experience of wonder. Voegelin often meditated on and quoted a passage from Aristotle's *Metaphysics* that links myth and philosophy through the experience of wonder and wondering:

2. Voegelin, "Autobiographical Statement at Age Eighty-Two," 451.

it is owing to their wonder that men both now begin and at first began to philosophize; they wondered originally at the obvious difficulties, then advanced little by little and stated difficulties about the greater matters. . . . And a man who is puzzled and wonders thinks himself ignorant (whence even the lover of myth [*philomythos*] is in a sense a lover of Wisdom [*philosophos*], for the myth is composed of wonders).[3]

Searching through the process of recollecting the experiences in his own consciousness, thereby implementing the Delphic-Socratic precept "Know thyself" that led to his life in philosophy, Voegelin conducted a set of anamnetic experiments in 1943. Describing these experiments to R. N. Palmer, editor of *Sewanee Review,* Voegelin observed "that the life of the spirit and intellect is historical in the strict sense, and that the determinants of mature philosophical speculation have to be sought in the *mythical formation of the mind in experiences of early youth.*"[4] Through these experiments, Voegelin was grounding his own philosophizing in the historical biography of his own consciousness. In the prefatory remarks to the first publication of these experiments in *Anamnesis* he asserts that "the radicalism of philosophizing can never be gauged either by the results or the critical framework of a system but rather, in a more literal sense, by the radices of philosophizing in the biography of philosophizing consciousness, i.e., *by the experiences that impel toward reflection and do so because they have excited consciousness to the 'awe' of existence.*"[5]

The importance of these anamnetic experiments lies in the connection Voegelin makes between the "mythical formation of the mind in the experiences of early youth" and the experiences that move the inchoate philosopher toward reflection because "they have excited consciousness to the 'awe' of existence." Myth was an integral component in the historical development of philosophy as the love of wisdom, especially in the work of Plato. Voegelin's own biographical experience demonstrated to him the foundation of philosophy in myth, itself "composed of wonders."

While Voegelin's early childhood experiences formed, shaped, and thus prepared him to become a philosopher, it was his adult experiences not only of the National Socialist forces of political disorder but also of the political turmoil of early twentieth-century Europe that motivated and guided the search for order that continued throughout his life. His

3. Aristotle *Metaphysics* 982b11–982b14, trans. Ross, p. 692.
4. Letter to J. N. Palmer, November 5, 1946, in Hoover Archives, Voegelin Papers, box 36, folder 8. Emphasis added.
5. Voegelin, *Anamnesis,* 84. Emphasis added.

own resistance to disorder began with his recognition of the spiritual disease underlying Nazi racist theories, which led him to publish two books in the 1930s analyzing and critiquing these theories. After his flight from Vienna to America in 1938, he continued that search for order in a more congenial milieu as he worked on his History of Political Ideas. In *Autobiographical Reflections,* he said that "the motivations of my work, which culminates in a philosophy of history, are simple. They arise from the political situation." And he added: "Anybody with an informed and reflective mind who lives in the twentieth century since the end of the First World War, as I did, finds himself hemmed in, if not oppressed, from all sides by a flood of ideological language."[6] In the process of mastering the primary material for the History of Political Ideas project, Voegelin discovered, especially in the work of Plato, that philosophy itself was developed as a response to the political and spiritual disorder of Athenian society. In *Plato and Aristotle,* he argued that

> The philosopher is compactly the man who resists the sophist; the man who attempts to develop right order in his soul through resistance to the diseased soul of the sophist; the man who can evoke a paradigm of right social order in the image of his well-ordered soul, in opposition to the disorder of society that reflects the disorder of the sophist's soul; the man who develops the conceptual instruments for the diagnosis of health and disease in the soul; the man who develops the criteria of right order, relying on the divine measure to which his soul is attuned.[7]

Of course political and social disorder may provoke various types of resistance, and resistance does not necessarily become a philosophical search for order. That Voegelin's resistance took the form of a philosophical search originated with those experiences of early childhood that he later remembered had excited his "consciousness to the 'awe' of existence." This experience of the awe of existence resembles the primary experience of the cosmos that is equivalent to a faith in the order of the cosmos and that is expressed, in the Christian symbolization, as faith. Voegelin's late work confirms this pattern of a fundamental faith in order, for there he becomes more attentive to the work of Anselm of Canterbury and his *fides quaerens intellectum.* In fact, in his very last

6. Voegelin, *Autobiographical Reflections,* 93.
7. Voegelin, *Plato and Aristotle,* 123. Voegelin's recognition of the importance of what he calls the "Platonic Anthropological Principle"—the state is man writ large—leads to some of his most important and insightful work on the nature of consciousness. His 1943 "anamnetic experiments" lay the groundwork for *Anamnesis.*

work, "Quod Deus Dicitur," Voegelin meditates in his final ascent to the divine upon the theme of his faith in search of understanding.

In volumes II and III of *Order and History* (*The World of the Polis* and *Plato and Aristotle*), Voegelin traces the history of the search for order from myth—the cosmological form that symbolizes experiences of order—through the development of philosophy in the work of the pre-Socratic philosophers, the Greek dramatists, and the Greek historians, culminating in the work of Plato and Aristotle. He observed that in this development the philosophers (especially Plato and Aristotle), rather than rejecting mythical symbolizations, recognized that there existed in myth an essential kinship with philosophy and an indispensable component—an experience of wonder—without which philosophy could not proceed. In his later work especially, Voegelin identified this component as a "primary experience of the cosmos." This insight into the history of the search for order enabled Voegelin to differentiate the components of philosophy that recognized the vital role of mythical symbolizations in the philosophical quest to understand and to symbolize the experiences of order with greater precision and insight.[8] Thus, Voegelin's historical researches confirmed for him empirically what he had discovered in his own particular case, that is, that the experiences of order symbolized mythically were an indispensable foundational element of the philosophical search for order. Not only, then, does philosophy have a double origin—historically in the human search for order and biographically in the person of the philosopher—but philosophical understanding itself reveals the double-ness of its empirical grounding.

### EXPERIENCE: THE EMPIRICAL GROUNDING OF PHILOSOPHY

The double empirical grounding of Voegelin's philosophy is built upon the experiential exploration of the depths of the philosopher's own psyche and upon the search of order experienced and symbolized in literary documents of the past—Hesiod's poems, Heraclitus's fragments, Plato's dialogues, the Torah, or the Gospels, for example. In a letter to Heilman, Voegelin explained that in composing *Anamnesis: On the Theory of History and Politics,* he had empirically grounded his work by organizing it around meditations—explorations of his consciousness

8. Voegelin, *In Search of Order.*

in the Heraclitean depth[9]—and historical studies. He pointed out that
he had included two meditations, in the first and third parts. The first
meditation, which he conducted and wrote down in 1943, enabled him
to recover "consciousness from the current theories of consciousness,
especially from Phaenomenology." The second meditation he conducted in 1965 through a "rethinking of the Aristotelian exegesis of
consciousness (in *Met.* I and II)," and then expanding "into new areas
of consciousness that had not come within the ken of classic philosophy
but must be explored now, in order to clear consciousness" of current
dogmatisms. Between these two meditations he had placed in part II,
"Experience and History," which contained studies that "demonstrate
how the historical phenomena of order give rise to the type of analysis
which culminates in the meditative exploration of consciousness." He
concluded that "the whole book is held together by a double movement
of empiricism" (letter 110, June 19, 1966, pp. 242–43).

To illustrate the nature of these meditations, which he referred to as
"a new literary form in philosophy" (ibid., p. 241), Voegelin wrote:

> At present, we are faced with the problem of getting rid of a considerable
> heap of dogma—theological, metaphysical, and ideological—and to
> recover the original experiences of man's tension toward the divine
> ground of his existence. Now, while dogma can be presented in the form
> of systems, of ratiocination from unquestioned premises, or discursive
> exposition of problems presented in the philosophical literature, original
> exegesis of consciousness can proceed only by the form of direct obser-
> vation and meditative tracing of the structure of the psyche. Moreover,
> this structure is not a given to be described by means of propositions, but
> a process of the psyche itself that has to find its language symbols as it
> proceeds. And finally, the self-interpretation of consciousness cannot be
> done once for all, but is a process in the life-time of a human being. . . .
> The exegesis is an attempt to recover or remember, (hence the title
> *Anamnesis*), the human condition revealing itself in consciousness, when
> it is smothered by the debris of opaque symbols. (ibid., p. 242)

What is especially important for our study is both that Voegelin's
"double movement of empiricism" focuses on experiences—engendering experiences—and the symbolizations of these experiences, and that
the validation-confirmation of Voegelin's empiricism can only occur in
the consciousness of the reader. One of the most succinct assessments

---

9. Heraclitus Fragment B101: I searched into myself.

of Voegelin's emphasis upon human experience as the empirical foundation of philosophy comes from a leading Voegelin scholar, Ellis Sandoz. In his introduction to *Published Essays, 1966–1985*, he writes:

> The key [to re-establishing a theoretical science of humanity that would include all dimensions of human existence] lies in distinguishing the modes and scope of experience and in keeping in mind that experience is a transaction in consciousness. At the level of common sense, it is evident that human beings have experiences other than sensory perceptions, and it is equally evident that philosophers like Plato and Aristotle explored reality on the basis of experiences far removed from perception. The Socratic "Look and see if this is not the case" does not invite one to survey public opinion but asks one to descend into the psyche, that is, to search reflective consciousness. Moreover, it is evident that the primarily nonsensory modes of experience address dimensions of human existence superior in rank and worth to those sensory perception does: experiences of the good, beautiful, and just, of love, friendship, and truth, of all human virtue and vice, and of divine reality. Apperceptive experience is distinguishable from sensory perception and a philosophical science of substance from a natural science of phenomena. Experience of "things" is modeled on the subject-object dichotomy of perception in which the consciousness intends the object of cognition. But such a model of experience and knowing is ultimately insufficient to explain the operations of consciousness with respect to the nonphenomenal reality men approach in moral, aesthetic, and religious experiences. . . .
>
> The participatory (*metaleptic*) experiences of human beings in the In-Between (*metaxy*), which are the constitutive core of human reality, are transactions conducted within consciousness itself and not externally in time and space; hence Voegelin sometimes calls the realm in which they occur nonexistent reality . . . , or the realm of spirit.[10]

One should bear in mind that the findings of Voegelin's meditations and historical research are testable by any person who in loving openness to his own humanity and reality accepts the Socratic invitation to "Look and see if this is not the case."

We will recall that one of the motivations for Voegelin's philosophy—and for all philosophy—was the experience of political disorder and the desire to understand the nature of political disorder and, thereby, to search for the source of political order. In seeking to understand the political disorder that he experienced, Voegelin focused on the

---

10. Sandoz, Editor's Introduction to *Published Essays, 1966–1985*, by Voegelin, xx.

discovery made by Plato that the "state is man writ large." Voegelin called this the Platonic Anthropological Principle and developed Plato's insight by reflecting and meditating on what it means to be human. His meditations led him to focus on the nature of consciousness—as it is embodied in human beings who live in the *metaxy*, the In-Between. In the foreword to *Anamnesis*, Voegelin wrote that "the problems of human order in society and history originate in the order of consciousness. Hence the philosophy of consciousness is the centerpiece of a philosophy of politics."[11] There he briefly outlined his studies of theories of consciousness, the phenomena of order, "the reduction of the phenomena of order to the logos of consciousness" and the results of these studies. "The most important result of these efforts," he continued,

> was the insight that a "theory" of consciousness in the sense of generically valid propositions concerning a pre-given structure was impossible. For consciousness is not a given to be deduced from outside but an experience of participation in the ground of being whose logos has to be brought to clarity through the meditative exegesis of itself. The illusion of a "theory" had to give way to the reality of the meditative process; and this process had to go through its phases of increasing experience and insight.[12]

Thus, Voegelin's philosophy focuses on consciousness as the essence of human nature. Even if we call it the essence of human nature, consciousness cannot be reduced to a set of describable and objectively verifiable characteristics.

Voegelin's "double movement of empiricism" is very important not only for our study of literature through the lens provided by Voegelin's philosophy but also—and perhaps even more essentially—for the understanding of Voegelin's work itself. Only through "the dialogue that goes on among men about their nature and destiny" can philosophical findings on the order of those discovered by a Plato or a Voegelin be substantiated. And this substantiation can be accomplished only through the participation of "readers" in the reality adduced in the symbolizations of the philosophical works themselves. In other words, the validation-confirmation of the results of Voegelin's meditative experiences, as well as the validation of his historical studies—whether of Plato's texts or the fragments of Heraclitus or the Gospels or Homer or the Pentateuch—is a potentiality in the consciousness of every human

11. Voegelin, *Anamnesis*, 33.
12. Ibid.

being who lives and reads. And so it is with the validation-confirmation
of experiences that novels symbolize. It is in this context that the principles of Voegelin's literary criticism become important.

The bases for this validation-confirmation across the ages by readers
of literary works lie in what Voegelin—arguing against historicism and
relativism in a 1956 letter to Heilman—called "circumstanced equality."
He asserted: "All men are on the same level of circumstanced equality"
(letter 65, August 22, 1956, p. 158). While to be equally circumstanced
obviously means that all human beings are "located" in the same set of
circumstances, it is possible to describe with more specificity these circumstances that have been in fact discovered in Voegelin's own historical and personal search of order. The reader should be cautioned that
the following characteristics are empirically, i.e., experientially, verifiable only through the reflective-meditative process of embodied human
beings who, avoiding preconceptions, are open to the exploration of
consciousness. Thus we present these "circumstances," in which all
humans are equal, as "results" of the millennial "dialogue among men
about their nature and destiny":

> All human beings are born into an existence in time that is shared by
> "other" being things.
> All human beings born into existence will cease to exist in time.
> All human beings possess consciousness.
>   Consciousness participates in the nonexistent "ground of being."
> All human beings possess bodies.
>   Bodies participate in the existent world.
> The human body is the "location" of consciousness.
> Human beings are composite beings.

"To exist," as Voegelin observed,

> means to participate in two modes of reality: (1) in the Apeiron as the
> timeless *arche* of things and (2) in the ordered succession of things as the
> manifestation of the Apeiron in time. This dual participation of things in
> reality has been expressed by Heraclitus (fl. 500 B.C.) in the terse lan-
> guage of the mysteries (B62):

> > Immortals mortals
> > mortals immortals
> > live the others' death
> > the others' life die.

Reality in the mode of existence is experienced as immersed in reality in the mode of nonexistence and, inversely, nonexistence reaches into existence. The process has the character of an In-Between reality, governed by the tension of life and death.[13]

Because human consciousness experiences reality through participation in the timeless (nonexistent) ground of being and because through the body human beings participate in the existent world of time, human beings live in and are conscious of living in the *metaxy*—the In-Between of reality. Like coming into and going out of existence, the experience of the *metaxy* is shared by human beings across time and space.

## "God and Man, World and Society Form a Primordial Community of Being"

This simple declaration from "Introduction: The Symbolization of Order" in *Israel and Revelation*[14] opens the first major theoretical statement of Voegelin's philosophical principles following *The New Science of Politics*. It expresses both the empirical results of his historical researches and the announcement of the philosophical project that ceased only with his death.

Human beings *participate* in all the levels of reality—the community of being—to which they are granted access by their composite *human* nature. Participation (*methexis*—the Platonic participation in the Idea—and *metalepsis*—the Aristotelian mutual human-divine participation in the Nous) in the community of being is an essential component in Voegelin's philosophy. Although in *The New Science of Politics* (1952) Voegelin understands this participation to be primarily cognitive, as early as 1943 he had written of the participation as more than cognitive. This earlier formulation would only be published in 1966 and is consistent with work written much later and included in *Anamnesis*. The two passages from 1952 and 1943/1966 follow. In *The New Science of Politics* we read that

---

13. Voegelin, *Ecumenic Age,* 233. Sandoz points out in the Glossary of Terms Used in Eric Voegelin's Writings that he often used the *apeiron*—meaning the boundless or depth—"to refer to the pole of the *metaxy* standing opposite the One, or the Beyond." See Voegelin, *Autobiographical Reflections,* 151.

14. Voegelin, "Introduction: The Symbolization of Order," in *Israel and Revelation,* 39.

science starts from the prescientific existence of man, from his participation in the world with his body, soul, intellect, and spirit, from his primary grip on all the realms of being that is assured to him because his
own nature is their epitome. And from this *primary cognitive participation,* turgid with passion, rises the arduous way, the *methodos,* toward the
dispassionate gaze on the order of being in the theoretical attitude.[15]

In "On the Theory of Consciousness" we read:

> Human consciousness is not a process that occurs in the world in isola-
> tion, in contact with other processes only through cognition; rather, it is
> based on animal, vegetative, and inorganic being, and only on this basis
> is it the consciousness of a human being. This structure of being seems
> to be the ontic premise for man's ability to transcend himself toward the
> world, for in none of its directions of transcending does consciousness
> find a level of being that is not also one on which it itself is based.
> Speaking ontologically, consciousness finds in the order of being of the
> world no level that it does not also experience as its own foundation. In
> the "base-experience" of consciousness man presents himself as an epit-
> ome of the cosmos, as a microcosm. Now we do not know in what this
> base "really" consists; all our finite experience is experience of levels of
> being in their differentiation; the nature of their connections is inexpe-
> rienceable, whether this nexus be the foundation of the vegetative in the
> inorganic, of the animal in the vegetative, or of human consciousness in
> the animal body. There is no doubt, however, *that* this base exists. Even
> though each level of being is clearly distinguishable with its own struc-
> ture, there must be something common that makes their continuum in
> human existence possible.[16]

### REALITY-LANGUAGE-IMAGINATION

As he continued to study consciousness in the 1980s, Voegelin
began to reflect on the complex of reality, language, and consciousness.
In these reflections he identified "thing-reality" and "It-reality" as structures of reality that correspond to "intentionality" and "luminosity" in
consciousness. That these structures "cannot be separated as entities but
are together in the one structure of consciousness" he termed "the

15. Voegelin, *New Science of Politics,* 91–92. Emphasis added.
16. Voegelin, "On the Theory of Consciousness," in *Anamnesis,* 75–76. Even though
this passage was written in 1943, it would not be published until 1966 in *Anamnesis. Zur
Theorie der Geschichte und Politik.*

*paradox of consciousness.*"[17] In *In Search of Order* the paradoxes of consciousness continued to unfold in consciousness as "a subject intending reality as its object, but at the same time a something in a comprehending [It] reality; and reality is the object of consciousness, but at the same time the subject of which consciousness is to be predicated."[18] Voegelin had articulated in "The Beyond and Its Parousia" (1982) "a further structure in consciousness: We can reflectively distance ourselves from the paradox in which we are involved and talk about it—and such talk is called *philosophy.* I call this structure of consciousness *reflective distance.* All philosophy is conducted in reflective distance within consciousness about consciousness." This observation led directly to the insight that "such talk" was only one of the "three levels of language, which are in conflict with [one another]: the thing-reality language, the It-reality language, and the reflective distance language."[19]

In his last work, Voegelin described imagination as part of the structure of reality. He argued that reality is imaginative and thus must be apperceived imaginatively. Here he discovered that "the paradox of consciousness governs imagination, too":

> Imagination, as a structure in the process of a reality that moves toward its truth, belongs both to human consciousness in its bodily location and to the reality that comprehends bodily located man as a partner in the community of being. There is no truth symbolized without man's imaginative power to find the symbols that will express his response to the appeal of reality; but there is no truth to be symbolized without the comprehending It-reality in which such structures as man with his participatory consciousness, experiences of appeal and response, language, and imagination occur. Through the imaginative power of man the It-reality moves imaginatively toward its truth.[20]

Even though Voegelin does not use the term *cognitive* in this declaration about the imaginative structure of the It-reality and the corresponding imaginative structure of human consciousness, his emphasis upon the "truth" of the symbols as "cognitive" in the questions he asks himself in

---

17. Voegelin, "The Beyond and Its Parousia," in *The Drama of Humanity,* 398–99.
18. Voegelin, *In Search of Order,* 30–31.
19. Voegelin, "The Beyond and Its Parousia," 399.
20. Voegelin, *In Search of Order,* 52. And just as there are no free-floating consciousnesses, unmoored from specific human bodies with specific, biographically (i.e., historically) formed personalities, there are no imaginations floating free of specific, embodied persons.

order to arrive at the declaration itself leads us to conclude that this structure might be named the "cognitive-imaginative." In his essay "Wisdom and the Magic of the Extreme," Voegelin wrote that the "the truth of the symbols is not informative; it is evocative."[21] Since "truth of the symbols" is "evocative," it seems apparent that the evocation of the *truth* of the symbols will necessarily involve the imagination. We feel justified, therefore, in naming this structure in consciousness and in the It-reality that makes evocation possible the "cognitive-imaginative."[22] This does not seem to be inconsistent with Voegelin's understanding of symbolization, truth, and evocation.

Imagination in both of its dimensions—as a structural human capacity and as a structural element of It-reality—is the key to the literary critic's enterprise. As part of the structure of reality, imagination characterizes the nonexistent dimension of the It-reality that is experienceable through the imaginative dimension of the consciousness of embodied human beings in the *metaxy,* because the human imagination is related to the imagination of the It-reality. Through imagination, man participates in the imaginative dimension of the It-reality and hence of the community of Being. As a human capacity, imagination enables a particular human person, an embodied historical consciousness, to experience the imaginative dimension of reality and to find a way to symbolize that experience in order to articulate and to communicate that experience to others.[23]

I refer the reader now to Diagram A. In it I have tried (with apologies to Voegelin) to symbolize his philosophical insights, insofar as they are relevant to my focus on literature and literary interpretation. The diagram "reduces" the "cognitive-imaginative" acts of writing and reading to linear processes that cannot in reality be so reduced; for in an embodied human being who exists in the *metaxy,* there is a fluidity of movement within the community of being in which the person is an embodied participant. The transcendence of consciousness into reality and the penetration of external reality into consciousness is ultimately an irreducibly mysterious process. Only for convenience of discussing the activities of writing and reading attendant to the Literary Symbolization have we so "reduced" these acts to a diagrammatic form.

---

21. Voegelin, "Wisdom and the Magic of the Extreme," 344.
22. In the context of his discussion of Plato's "true story" in book I of the *Laws,* Voegelin writes: "The truth of reality, answering and questioning, arises in consciousness through the interaction of vision and noesis" (ibid., 337).
23. See "Imagination" in the glossary.

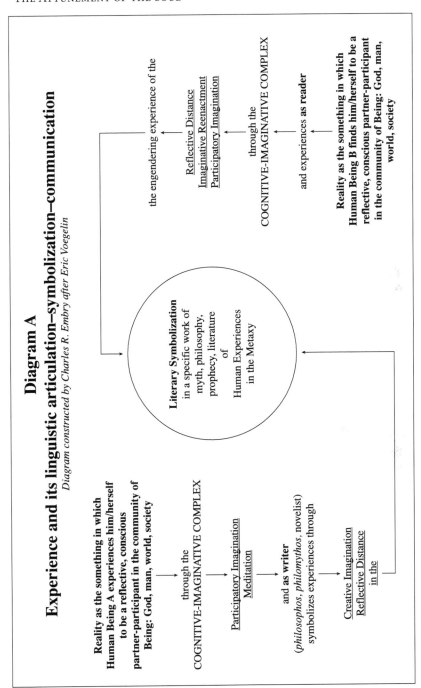

# Diagram A
## Experience and its linguistic articulation–symbolization–communication
*Diagram constructed by Charles R. Embry after Eric Voegelin*

Reality as the something in which
Human Being A experiences him/herself
to be a reflective, conscious
partner-participant in the community of
Being: God, man, world, society

through the
COGNITIVE-IMAGINATIVE COMPLEX

Participatory Imagination
Meditation

and **as writer**
(*philosophos, philomythos,* novelist)
symbolizes experiences through

Creative Imagination
Reflective Distance
in the

**Literary Symbolization**
in a specific work of
myth, philosophy,
prophecy, literature
of
Human Experiences
in the Metaxy

the engendering experience of the

Reflective Distance
Imaginative Reenactment
Participatory Imagination

through the
COGNITIVE-IMAGINATIVE COMPLEX

and experiences **as reader**

Reality as the something in which
Human Being B finds him/herself to be a
reflective, conscious partner-participant
in the community of Being: God, man,
world, society

Reading the chart is simple: Starting at the top left, one reads down, and from the bottom right one proceeds up. You will note that Human Being A and Human Being B exist "on the same level of circumstanced equality" as a "partner-participant in the community of Being." Thus the only thing that distinguishes Human Being A from Human Being B is their relationship to a literary work—A as writer and B as reader; and, of course, the writer is also a reader and the reader may also become a writer-interpreter. The "intent" of the writer is to express in language the reality of experience, while the "intent" of the reader is to experience the symbolization of the literary work in such a way as to permit the literary work to evoke the reality symbolized.

Reading from the top left down, the diagram specifies the act of Human Being A writing a Literary Symbolization. The COGNITIVE-IMAGINATIVE COMPLEX of the writer includes "Participatory Imagination," "Meditation," "Creative Imagination," and "Reflective Distance" as components of the writer. I placed "Creative Imagination" and "Reflective Distance" between the "Human Being as writer" and "Literary Symbolization" in order to distinguish the "tools" that the writer uses to "produce" a literary work from the dimensions of consciousness that supports the writer's experiences in the *metaxy*. The entire complex of components from the top left through the "Reflective Distance" of the writer should be associated with the "creator" of the Literary Symbolization.

As one reads from the bottom right up, the diagram focuses on the act of reading aimed at permitting the Literary Symbolization to evoke in the reader the reality, the experience of which is symbolized in the literary work itself. Again the entire complex of components from the bottom right up through the "Reflective Distance" of the reader should be understood as the "reader" of the Literary Symbolization. Although the writer's and reader's realities are the same—they are on the "same level of circumstanced equality"—since its creation, the Literary Symbolization has now become part of the reality of both. Since the Literary Symbolization has become part of reality, the reader finds it both as a component of reality and as a symbolization that attracts his interest in understanding it. This initial attraction by the Literary Symbolization then leads the reader into the adventure—through the engagement of his "cognitive-imaginative" skills—of seeking to understand the Symbolization itself. If the reader is, moreover, intent not only on reading and hence on understanding the Symbolization, he will engage his skills with the further aim of "seeing through" the

Symbolization to the reality from which it emerged into the consciousness of the writer.

The truth of the symbols, of course, is not always readily apparent. Sometimes, in my own experience at least, the truth of the literary symbols must be actively pursued through the various dimensions of reading. I think that Voegelin invested vast cognitive-imaginative-meditative energies into his reading of literary texts. Athanasios Moulakis, in his introduction to *The World of the Polis,* argues that, like Marsilio Ficino, who enjoined the readers of Plato's dialogue *Parmenides* "to adopt a Platonic frame of mind" in approaching it, Voegelin "invites his reader to a *pia interpretatio* of the decisive documents, which does not mean the recognition of external authority or verities to be accepted on faith, but an inner preparation, a participatory disposition of the interpreter."[24] Only when the reader-interpreter participates in the Literary Symbolization does the symbol yield up its truth, for the symbolization embodied in the literary work exists, not in the "external world," but in the "existential movement in the *metaxy*" of the human being from whom it mysteriously emerged.[25] Thus the meaning of the symbolization lies, not at the level of semantic understanding, but only in the reenactment of the symbolized reality in the "existential movement in the *metaxy*" of the human being who "reads" the text. If the reading succeeds, the truth of the symbol has thus evoked the reality symbolized and has thereby drawn the reader into "the loving quest of truth."

24. Moulakis, Editor's Introduction to *The World of the Polis,* 24.

25. I want to emphasize that this mode of reading does *not* depend upon nor does it advocate a methodological stance such as the suspension of disbelief or an a priori procedural assumption of belief, but rests upon an existential stance that is consequent to the primary cosmic experience of an embodied human consciousness that experiences a cosmic order preceding the search for an understanding of order.

## 3

# Writer, Reader, and the Adventure of Participatory Consciousness

Someone loves Rembrandt, but seriously—that man will know that there is a God, he will surely believe it. . . . Somebody has followed maybe for a short time a free course at the great university of misery, and has paid attention to the things he sees with his eyes, and hears with his ears, and has thought them over; he, too, will end believing, and he will perhaps have learned more than he can tell. To try to understand the real significance of what the great artists, the serious masters, tell us in their masterpieces, that leads to God. One man has written or told it in a book, another in a picture. Well, think much and think all the time; that unconsciously raises your thoughts above the ordinary level. We know how to read—well, let us read then!

~ VINCENT VAN GOGH, *Dear Theo*

---

"The truth of the symbols is not informative; it is evocative."[1]

What does this straightforward, declarative, sentence mean? Prima facie it means that symbolic truth cannot be reduced to an informational statement about objective thing-reality but must instead exercise such an existential impact upon the reader of the symbolic work that the consciousness of the reader is reformed and enlightened. In his elaboration of this statement, Voegelin writes that

---

1. Voegelin, "Wisdom and the Magic of the Extreme," 344.

The symbols do not refer to structures in the external world but to the existential movement in the *metaxy* from which they mysteriously emerge as the exegesis of the movement in intelligibly expressive language. Their meaning can be said to be understood only if they have evoked in the listener or reader the corresponding movement of participatory consciousness. Their meaning, thus, is not simply a matter of semantic understanding; one should rather speak of their meaning as optimally fulfilled when the movement they evoke in the recipient consciousness is intense and articulate enough to form the existence of its human bearer and to draw him, in his turn, into the loving quest of truth.[2]

Looking closely at this statement, found in Voegelin's discussion of the mythical symbols expressed by Plato in the *Laws,* we can identify several emphases. The first sentence reads:

The symbols do not refer to structures in the external world but to the existential movement in the *metaxy* from which they mysteriously emerge as the exegesis of the movement in intelligibly expressive language.

This sentence draws attention to the fact that the Platonic symbols "mysteriously emerge" from "the existential movement in the *metaxy*" intelligibly to express in language the existential movement itself; the "existential movement" occurs as the result of participation of a human consciousness in the encompassing nonexistent It-reality. The symbols thus arise out of the *metaxy* experienced by a particular embodied consciousness, in this case the person Plato, who participates in the nonexistent It-reality. While all of us live in the *metaxy*—the spatio-metaphorical place where human consciousnesses exist—and share the common world of the *metaxy* as the condition of our humanity, there is no *metaxy* except as experienced in the consciousness of individuals. The symbols themselves, therefore, refer to the existential movement in the consciousness from which they mysteriously emerge; this emergence is not specifiable as to particulars and is essentially inexplicable. The most that can be said about the emergence of literary symbols itself is that it happens and that its happening is mysterious. To generalize, symbols are the literary indices, mysterious though their emergence may be, of participation in the reality of the cosmos in the soul of an embodied human being.

The second sentence reads:

2. Ibid., 344.

> Their meaning can be said to be understood only if they have evoked in
> the listener or reader the corresponding movement of participatory con-
> sciousness.

Since the symbols emerge in consequence of a movement in the consciousness of a human being as creator (in participation with the mysterious It-reality), they can only be "understood" if they elicit a
"corresponding" movement of participation in a reader's own participatory consciousness.

The third sentence reads:

> Their meaning, thus, is not simply a matter of semantic understanding;
> one should rather speak of their meaning as optimally fulfilled when the
> movement they evoke in the recipient consciousness is intense and artic-
> ulate enough to form the existence of its human bearer and to draw him,
> in his turn, into the loving quest of truth.

The meaning that inheres in literary symbols must extend beyond mere
semantic understanding of the symbols themselves to produce in the
"recipient consciousness"—the reader—an intense affective response
that re-forms the existence of the reader, re-calls his "understanding" of
his own nature as a human being and of the nature of the reality of
which he is a part and in which he participates, and enlightens his consciousness and draws him into the philosophical search for understanding. The literary symbols do not then need to communicate-transmit
the specific experience that gave rise to the particular literary symbols
(this is virtually impossible), but they must *affect* the reader in such a
powerful way as to stimulate a "loving quest" for the truth of existence.

Because all human beings are "on the same level of circumstanced
equality," because all human beings live in the *metaxy,* because human
nature is composite, participation in reality inevitably characterizes all
human endeavors, including philosophy and literature, writing and
reading. Participation in reality and the "circumstanced equality" of all
human beings extends, moreover, not only to human endeavors but
also to the products of human endeavors such as novels or meditations.

It is *from* the *metaxy* of a particular human being as writer participating in the mysterious It-reality that literary symbols emerge as a
result of an existential movement in the participant. The truth of literary symbols themselves is tinged with their origin in the *metaxy* of a
participatory consciousness, for literary symbolizations only exist as

dead letters with the potential for evoking a movement in the *metaxy* of a reader. And only if they summon in the reader a corresponding existential movement can the literary symbols be understood as meaningful. If a literary symbol is read literally, or only for semantic meaning with the expectation that it refers to a segment of objective reality with extension in space of the material and organic cosmos in which man participates with his body, the truth of the symbol will be missed.

Throughout this work, we have assumed, and argued, that literary works are symbolic; that a novel is a symbolic work; and that, therefore, the truth of the novel is evocative, not informative. The evocation of meaning, moreover, will only occur when there is a participation in the symbolic work that leads to the experience of participation in the cosmos in the *metaxy* of the reader's consciousness. In order for the novel to elicit such an existential movement in the consciousness of the reader, the reader must engage with intention in a reenactment of the symbolic complex that is the novel.

To demonstrate in a graphic form the various relationships among Reality, Consciousness, and the Novel discussed in the foregoing paragraphs, I call your attention to Diagram B and the subsequent explication.[3]

If the diagram is read by column from left to right, it becomes intelligible as a representation of the structures and symbolizations of each of the "realities" and the relationships among them, provided we recognize that REALITY encompasses within itself CONSCIOUSNESS and its product, NOVEL. The "Structures of" REALITY, CONSCIOUSNESS, and NOVEL are presented in each column and shared by the three "realities." In the application of the diagram in our discussion, CONSCIOUSNESS must be understood always as referring to an embodied consciousness of an individual human being, and NOVEL must be understood as always referring to a specific novel as the expression of the consciousness of a novelist. Finally, the relationships among the three "realities" are established and maintained through the Participatory Imagination of an embodied human being; the Participatory Imagination represents the faculty of a human being, of CONSCIOUSNESS, to experience and thus to "know" REALITY.

*Participatory Imagination 1:* CONSCIOUSNESS (of an embodied human being) participates in REALITY cognitively (through noetic

---

3. This diagram should be read in conjunction with Diagram A and should be understood as a more detailed rendering of some of the same elements.

rationality), imaginatively ("participatory imagination"), and through Intentionality and Luminosity.

As I have argued in the previous chapter, even though Voegelin does not formulate the term *participatory imagination* in order to designate the "faculty" that he uses in approaching literary texts, the term helps us understand both the human capacity that enables an individual to experience reality and the structure in human CONSCIOUSNESS that enables the reader of NOVELS (literary symbols) to reenact in his own CONSCIOUSNESS the experience that is preserved in the symbols of REALITY. Note that the "participatory imagination" also provides the "faculty" through which a human being participates in the It-reality. The "participatory imagination" enables a reader years and even millennia hence to glimpse through imaginative reenactment the engendering experiences symbolized in the language of the individual who originally experienced "participation in the cosmos."[4] Thus the "participatory imagination" is the structure in consciousness that not only enables one to symbolize an experience of the It-reality but also permits access to the It-reality via the linguistic symbolizations of previous engendering experiences.

Participation of CONSCIOUSNESS in REALITY occurs in the various structures of REALITY; thus, participation may be in any dimension of REALITY—the cosmic community of being symbolized in myth, OR the immanent or Transcendent levels of Reality of the Noetic/Pneumatic symbolizations OR the thing-reality or It-reality of Voegelin's late differentiation. Note that all symbolizations of REALITY in the diagram are equivalent.

*Participatory Imagination 2:* The participation of the CONSCIOUSNESS of the writer in REALITY through Participation 1 issues in imaginative symbolizations of the experiences of participation whether they be Platonic dialogues, Gospels, epics, meditations, or literary works— poems, novels, plays. A reader, however, imaginatively participates via Participation 2 in the literary symbolizations. This imaginative participation in the imaginative literary symbols directs or focuses the reader back to the experience of participation that has been symbolized by the writer. Thus a participatory reading will reenact an experience (as a "transaction in consciousness") of the reality symbolized.

*Participatory Imagination 3:* Imaginative symbolizations participate in REALITY insofar as they symbolize the experiences of CONSCIOUSNESS participating in REALITY. As such, they are both the

---

4. Voegelin, "Conversations," 290.

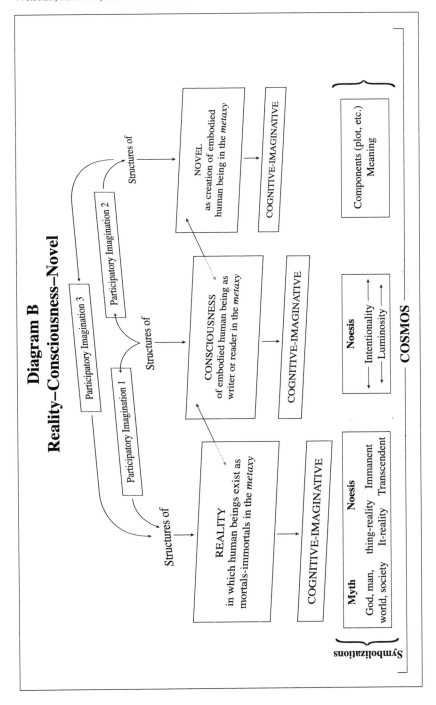

**Diagram B**
**Reality–Consciousness–Novel**

vehicles of a writer's expressions and guides pointing back toward the experiences that gave rise to them. The truth of imaginative symbolizations is evocative of the experience and may, under the right circumstances (such as the participation—cognitive and imaginative—of a reader's consciousness in the experience to which the symbolizations point or express) elicit in the reader qualities of the experience mediated by the imaginative symbolization.

The Structures of REALITY—as experienced and symbolized by concrete human beings—reveal REALITY itself to be "constituted" of:

a. the compact Cosmos: God, man, world, and society in the symbolization of Myth.

b. the differentiated Cosmos: the Transcendent (the divine) and immanent (the world—Nature, society, and man as an existent being in space-time) in the symbolizations of Philosophy (Noesis) and Revelation (Pneuma).

c. the Cosmos: thing-reality and It-reality as further differentiated inclusively of Myth, Philosophy, and Revelation in Noetic Philosophy as practiced and symbolized by Eric Voegelin.

The Structures of CONSCIOUSNESS as revealed in the participation of man in REALITY are experienced in the meditative process and symbolized as Intentionality (corresponding to thing-reality) and Luminosity (corresponding to It-reality). But since It-reality encompasses and forms thing-reality, CONSCIOUSNESS experiences It-reality in the Beingness of all the being things of thing-reality as well as in the divine ground of Being.

The Structures of NOVEL are cognitive-imaginative in nature and include the linguistic-organizational Components, on the one hand, and the Meaning that suffuses the analytically identifiable Components. In creating a "thing" called NOVEL, CONSCIOUSNESS (of the novelist) relies upon its Intentionality to construct or build a book that "contains" the novel. But because the literary expression or symbolization emerges mysteriously from the existential movement that takes place in the *metaxy* and because the symbolization relies upon linguistic tools such as grammar, syntax, and words with thing-reality referents, the parts of NOVEL analogically embody the Meaning. Meaning itself arises out of the Luminosity of CONSCIOUSNESS and its capacity both to experience the It-reality and to symbolize the experience even though it is submerged in the Components of the novel created by the rational Intentionality of the novelist's consciousness. Thus, the Time of the Tale, an analogue of creation itself, comes into being when the content and form merge as they do in NOVEL (and in myth).[5]

The NOVEL expresses the writer's experience of REALITY in one or more of its dimensions—God, man, world, and society OR immanent/transcendent reality OR thing-reality/It-reality. Participation characterizes the writer's experience of REALITY in one or more of its dimensions; the experience that is both cognitive and imaginative in turn shapes the linguistic symbolization. The writer through the intentionality of CONSCIOUSNESS "constructs" a NOVEL—just as an artist paints a picture or sculpts a sculpture—by relying upon the techniques of word-craft, which includes the components of the NOVEL such as plot, character development, action, exposition. The created tale or story of the NOVEL reveals through the imaginative dimension of the NOVEL the luminosity of experience—the experience of being in its thing-reality and its It-reality manifestations. When a tale includes the divine, cosmic, and human elements of REALITY, it rises to the status of Voegelin's Time of the Tale. Participation also characterizes the reader's experience of the symbolization—the NOVEL—that evokes the participation of the reader's own experience of Reality when the Socratic intent, "let us see if this is not so," is urged on, and accepted by, the reader.

In the preceding discussion, we sketched out the various dimensions of Participation as they are related to REALITY, to CONSCIOUSNESS, and to the NOVEL, as well as the ways in which REALITY, CONSCIOUSNESS, and the NOVEL are interrelated through the Participation of human beings. Thus, CONSCIOUSNESS (of an Embodied human being) is central to human experience in the In-Between (*metaxy*) of existence.

We are now in a position to ask: What does it mean to read, understand, and critique novels from within the framework of Voegelin's philosophy?

Above all a Voegelinian reading of literature depends upon participation, the participation of the human being in reality and in the symbolic constellation of the novel, and it aims at reenactment. Recall the statement by Moulakis that Voegelin "invites his reader to a *pia interpretatio* of the decisive documents, which does not mean the recognition of external authority or verities to be accepted on faith, but an inner preparation, a participatory disposition of the interpreter."[6] Sandoz also stressed participation by the reader of literature. In the epilogue to the second edition of his study of Dostoyevsky, he writes that "the readers

---

5. See chap. 1 for "Time of the Tale."
6. Moulakis, Editor's Introduction to *World of the Polis,* 24.

enter into the work itself as participants, and they do not emerge from it the same as they were before."[7] As we have emphasized throughout our discussion of Voegelin's literary criticism and philosophy, "participation" occupies a central role in all his work. The reader must be prepared, then, to participate in the novel, and this participation requires full engagement of the reader's nature as a human being—body, soul, intellect, imagination, and spirit—while relying upon the intentional and luminal dimensions of consciousness and exercising the cognitive-imaginative faculties of consciousness.

Moulakis observed that in Voegelin's mode of reading Plato, his "purpose was not to cull precepts from the past, but to reenact, at an advanced level of differentiation, Plato's response to the crisis of Athens. Reenactment meant taking to heart an exemplary lesson, which can only be properly understood by *being* reenacted, i.e., by reconstructing the motivating experiences behind the verbal and symbolic forms that have come down to us as documentary evidence."[8] Voegelin's mode of reading in order to reconstruct the "motivating experiences behind the verbal and symbolic forms" is applicable to other texts—like poems and novels—that document and symbolize experiences understood as "transactions in the consciousness" of the creator-writer. These experiences were identified by Robert Frost as adventures that happen to the poet:

> There are a lot of things I could say to you about the art [of poetry] if we were talking, and one of them is that it should be of major adventures only, outward or inward—important things that happen to you, or important things that occur to you. . . . I put the two on equal terms, the things that happen to you and the things that occur to you. You can't have them at will, but they are certainties now and then in any life of living and thinking. And when you get a good one, given out of nowhere, you can almost trust it to do itself in poetry. Almost, I say. You can at least seem to throw away all you ever learned in your long apprenticeship to formal beauty.[9]

To understand the adventure that generates a novel, the reader must penetrate to the "motivating experiences behind the verbal and symbolic forms"; in order to do so, the reader must reenact the experiences

---

7. Sandoz, *Political Apocalypse,* 276.
8. Moulakis, Editor's Introduction, 3.
9. R. Frost to Kimball Flacus, November 26, [1932?], in *Robert Frost on Writing,* by Berry, 111–12.

in and through the imaginative dimensions of his own consciousness. In order for this reenactment to occur, however, the reader must prepare himself existentially to be "persuaded" or "moved" by fiction in general, and by a specific novel in particular. I am reminded here of the question that Polemarchos puts to Socrates after Socrates avers that he could return to Athens if he could persuade Polemarchos and his friends to let him leave the Piraeus. Polemarchos asks: Could you persuade us if we refused to listen? Polemarchos knew that to be persuaded the hearer must first "adopt" an openness that includes a readiness to experience persuasion itself as a mysterious symbolization of an existential movement in the *metaxy* of his existence. In our times, this existential openness includes not only the "willingness to be moved by a novel" but also a willingness to be reminded that a nonexistent reality lies behind the visible reality of our daily world. Flannery O'Connor believed that "good fiction" can only be understood by "the kind of mind that is *willing* to have its sense of mystery deepened by contact with reality, and its sense of reality deepened by contact with mystery."[10] Essentially, a novel (or a myth or a Platonic dialogue) can evoke and transform the reader only if the reader relaxes his natural wariness about fiction and its unreal nowhereness and prepares a space midway between belief and skepticism; the reader simply must be open to letting the symbolization work its charm upon the body, intellect, imagination, soul, and spirit.

An open existence, as Voegelin calls it, is at once the precondition for reenactment and the consequence of evocation that results in reenactment. Existence in openness is complex, paradoxical, and mysterious, much like the philosophical search itself is mysterious. It is as though one were to command the reader: "Be open to what the novel has to teach you about yourself and the world in which you live," when in fact the only way to persuade the reader of the need for openness is to provide a reason for being open. Viktor Frankl observed that if you want a person to laugh you cannot command him to laugh, you must tell him a joke.[11] The novel in our discussion is analogous to the joke in Frankl's observation. So, while at one level evocation must begin with the reader's predisposition to openness before encountering the symbols in the novel, at another level the encounter with the novel's symbols is what must open the reader to its truth. Readers, like the interlocutors in

---

10. O'Connor, "Nature and Aim of Fiction," 79.
11. Frankl, *Man's Search for Meaning*, 162–63.

Plato's dialogues, must be moved to remember the mortal-immortal nature of their own existence as human beings. A novel that is any good will stimulate this memory. If the reader permits the novel to work, he will be reminded of the composite nature of his humanity and thereby invited into loving search for the truth of existence.

In addition to cultivating existential openness, a reader who confronts a difficult and complex novel must invest time and energy in the activities of reading, analysis, and imaginative-meditative submersion in the story. While it is not possible to describe these stages of engagement with any great degree of precision, it is through these activities that the reader participates in the novel as a symbolization that has mysteriously emerged from the existential movement in the *metaxy* of the novelist. At a practical level, I think that any worthwhile novel will demand at least three readings. The reader should (1) read the novel through once in an effort to "grok"[12] it as a whole; (2) re-read the novel with attention to its parts—plot, character development, chronology, etc.; (3) re-read the novel through a third time in recognition and restoration of its artistic wholeness in consciousness. These three readings are the most easily identifiable activities that constitute participatory reading; but while they may be specified, the imaginative and meditative "skills" upon which the reader relies to understand the novel experientially are mostly unspecifiable in detail. They can only be pointed to.

12. *Grok* is a technical term taken from a science fiction novel, *Stranger in a Strange Land,* by Robert Heinlein. It refers to a mode of understanding that includes rational-cognitive components as well as those thoughts that a man "thinks in the marrowbone" (W. B. Yeats, "A Prayer for Old Age").

# Part II

# The
# Storyteller

# 4

## The Barren Quest

### Graham Swift's *Waterland*

I shall begin from the Beginning, from the cosmos as it impresses itself on man by the splendor of its existence, by the movements of the starry heavens, by the intelligibility of its order, and by its lasting as the habitat of man. The man who receives the impression, in his turn is endowed with an intellect both questioning and imaginative.

~ ERIC VOEGELIN,
"THE BEGINNING AND THE BEYOND: A MEDITATION ON TRUTH"

For the invisible things of him from the creation of the world are clearly seen, being understood by the things that are made, *even* his eternal power and Godhead.

~ SAINT PAUL'S LETTER TO THE ROMANS (1:20)

---

Voegelin's philosophy is characterized above all by his recognition and exploration of the experiential sources from which arises the philosophical search for understanding the reality in which we exist as human beings. One of these sources is the experience of disorder and disarray that appears as a permanent component of human life, for not only does political, economic, social, and moral disorder characterize our time, the time of modernity, it characterizes all times. The quest for understanding the disorder and disarray of life is perennial, resulting historically in symbolizations of order. At no time, as Voegelin emphasizes in his essay "Equivalences of Experience and Symbolization in History," have human beings agreed upon "one set of true propositions" about the "truth of human existence."[1] Why? What has the quest for understanding yielded if not agreement upon a fundamental set of truth propositions about human existence? And why does the quest so often result, as Voegelin also suggests in this essay, in ideological dogmatism or skepticism?

Graham Swift's novel *Waterland* symbolizes the derailment of the quest into a self-conscious and knowing, yet helpless, skepticism. The story of *Waterland* is borne by the first-person narrative of Tom Crick, a comprehensive school history teacher in Cambridge, England, and historian, in the year 1980. While the novel relates a story set in the Fens ("Ours was the marsh country" reads one of the novel's epigraphs, taken from Dickens's *Great Expectations*), the metaphorical landscape of the story extends the reach of the novel to the horizons of the human condition and the world itself. The other epigraph (two definitions of *Historia, -ae*) announces to the reader the style of the narrative as both an inquiry and story or tale of past events. More specifically, the *Historia* style permits the narrator to reflect throughout his inquiry, like Herodotus, upon various topics of historical and philosophical interest. Thus Tom's comprehensive account simultaneously and intermittently narrates: events of the central story that occur in 1943; his search for an explanation of the antecedents (causes) and consequences (effects) of the 1943 events extending to the history of his ancestors; and reflections on human nature, history, storytelling, land reclamation, empire-building, Progress, the French Revolution, Natural History, Artificial History, and civilization. These elements are woven into a story that Tom tells students in his History A class. Although many of the fifty-two chapters bear directly on the events of 1943 and later events in Tom's life, other chapters focus on the histories of Tom's ancestors, recount incidents from the French Revolution, or contain short treatises on natural phenomena. The digressive chapters—self-contained mini-essays—require the reader to ponder their role in Tom's lecture, which he terms a complete and final version of the story of his imminent separation from his students, compelled by an early retirement. Take, for example, a chapter entitled "About the Ouse." The Great Ouse, the major river of the Fens of East Anglia, must be considered in any effort to make the Fens livable through the process of land reclamation. In this

---

1. Voegelin, "Equivalences of Experience," 117.

chapter, Tom muses on the prehistoric beginnings of the river Ouse, speculates on its relation to the ages of man, and comments on the statement by Heraclitus that no man can step into the same river twice. The reader is left to discover the relationship of the chapter's contents to the larger story that Tom is telling the children.

In 1980, the narrative present, Tom faces two problems: he has discerned in his students a fear for the future—theirs and humankind's—and Mary, his wife of thirty-three years, has stolen an untended child from a grocery in Lewisham. The first of these problems has led him to set aside the French Revolution (required by the school curriculum) and to begin telling stories to his class. The second has forced his early retirement from teaching. The story that Tom tells his students embeds the events of 1943 and his search for the explanation of these events in a vast historical context.

The contagion of fear among the students leads to their questioning the raison d'être of teaching history, because as his prized student Price—a student whom he will claim later as his own son—asserts, "what matters . . . is the here and now . . . and the future"[2] (W, 6). "The only important thing about history," Price continues, "is that it's got to the point where it's probably about to end" (W, 7). Beginning a valedictory that will conclude only with his speech at the retirement assembly,[3] Tom calls to his students:

> Children, who will inherit the world. Children to whom, throughout history, stories have been told, chiefly but not always at bedtime, in order to quell restless thoughts; whose need of stories is matched only by the need adults have of children to tell stories to, of receptacles for their stock of fairy-tales, of listening ears on which to unload those most unbelievable yet haunting of fairy-tales, their own lives; children—they are going to separate you and me. (W, 7–8)

Despite intentions to narrate a straightforward, historical tale of cause and effect, Tom can neither simply recount the events of 1943 nor easily explain these events that lead into his present. In his attempt to tell the complete and final version, Tom conflates the actions and consequences of his own story with those of the human story—of human actions and consequences and the search for a beginning of history

2. Since Graham Swift often uses ellipses in his writing, I will designate ellipses that appear in Swift's text as periods unseparated by spaces and ellipses that I insert in quotations as periods separated by spaces.

3. This speech is recorded in chapter forty-nine, "About Empire-building."

"where things go wrong; [because] history is born only with trouble, with perplexity, with regret" (*W,* 106). When those investigating Mary's theft of a baby say to him, "Look, sir, shall we go back to the beginning?" (*W,* 314), he replies:

> The beginning? But where's that? How far back is that? Very well, I confess that my wife, with intention so to do, took a baby from an unminded pram. Very well (this far back?): I confess my responsibility jointly with my wife, for the death of three people (that is—it's not so simple—one of them was never born, and one of them—who knows if it was really a death...). (*W,* 314)

In search of the beginning, Tom weaves together the various skeins of events that permit him to reflect upon Natural History and Artificial History and on man—the animal that asks why, the animal that tells stories, the animal that demands meaning—reflections that reach, in the valedictory to his children, to thoughts on empire-building and civilization.

Tom structures his study of history, his search for causes—and asks his students to do likewise—like one who is conducting an inquest. He then proceeds to describe a historical situation from the French Revolution that paralleled his own dilemma in 1943 when Freddie Parr's body floated down the Leem and bumped up against the Atkinson Lock; that is, he asks: What does one do when faced with a corpse? He says to his students:

> Suppose we have on our hands a corpse—viz., the past. . . . For example, the headless trunk of Louis XVI. . . . We ask: Why did this corpse come to be a corpse? Answer: By accident—or because on a certain day in Paris when a certain guillotine was descending, Louis XVI happened to have his neck in the way. . . .
>
> But why, we ask, did Louis' neck happen to be—? Because... And when we have gleaned that reason we will want to know, But why that reason? Because... And when we have that further reason, But why again—? Because... Why?... Because... Why?... Until, in order to find out why Louis died, it is necessary not only to reanimate in our imaginations his troubled life and times but even to penetrate the generations before him. (*W,* 107)

This passage describes precisely the procedure that Tom follows in seeking an explanation for the appearance of Freddie's corpse at his father's lock. He will reanimate in his imagination his own troubled life and times and expand his search in ever-widening circles to include the history of his ancestors the Atkinsons and the Cricks, their native habitat the Fens where water and land determine and limit human activity, and eventually (because of special circumstances) the scientific study of that emblem of the Fens—the European eel, *Anguilla anguilla*.

What at first appears to be an accidental drowning—everyone knows that Freddie Parr cannot swim—and what is later even ruled an accident at the coroner's inquest, turns out to be a murder. Thinking that the coroner's ruling had extricated him and Mary from blame, Tom became really scared when later the same day Mary said to him: "I told him it was Freddie. Dick [Crick] killed Freddie Parr because he thought it was him. Which means we're to blame too" (*W*, 35).

Why does Mary understand immediately that Freddie died at the hand of Dick Crick, Tom's older brother? What did she tell Dick? And why are she and Tom to blame? By July 1943, Tom, then age 16, had come to think that reality is "uneventfulness, vacancy, and flatness" (*W*, 40), but reality had now become eventful, for Mary was pregnant. Could Mary, however, know that the baby was Tom's? During that same summer she had been instructing Dick, a simple-minded boy who couldn't even learn to read, in the sentimental ways of "l-luv," all the while engaging in a purely sexual relationship with Freddie Parr on the side. Tom was in love with Mary Metcalf, despite his knowledge of her other sexual relationships. Therefore, in order to throw suspicion away from Tom, Mary told Dick that Freddie was the baby's father.

In search of the reasons for this tangle, Tom settles on Curiosity. "Curiosity," Tom tells his children later, "begets love. It weds us to the world. It's part of our perverse, madcap love for this impossible planet we inhabit. People die when curiosity goes. People have to find out, people have to know" (*W*, 206). And fifteen-year-old Mary was beyond restraint—she longed to touch, to look, to experience whatever was hidden from her (*W*, 51). Spurred by her curiosity and Tom's equally curious response, they explore each other's bodies that summer of 1943. Within the old windmill by the Hockwell Lode "everything is open, everything is plain. . . . Us Fenlanders do not try to hide—since we know God is watching . . . curiosity and innocence held hands . . . we first used those magic, those spell-binding words which make the empty world seem full, just as surely as a thing fits inside a hole: I love—I love—Love, love..." (*W*, 52). Curiosity, Tom observes to his students, is a vital force that compels us to arduous meditations, leads to the writing of history books, and occasionally leads to the terror of the

"Here and Now" as when on that fateful morning Freddie's body washed up at the Atkinson Lock.

Tom's involvement in Mary's curiosity to know carnal things originates with train rides home from their respective schools in Gildsey and in a group swim at the Hockwell Lode in 1940. In response to Mary's urgings of "Show us, show us," a group of young teenagers agreed to a game of tease and dare, during which the girls bared their breasts and the boys, except for Dick, dropped their swimming trunks. The game ended with Freddie Parr putting a live eel down Mary's knickers. Remembering these events, Tom tells his children:

> Your teacher notes, in true historically observant fashion, the look that Dick directs (after first looking at the eel) at Mary. . . . He notes how Dick looks at Mary and then how Mary looks at Dick; and he notes how Freddie Parr catches both these looks which Dick and Mary give each other.
> And in all this looking at others' looks he too has a look of his own. . . . Because your history teacher (though he's never told her) is in love, it's a fact, with Mary Metcalf. (*W*, 207)

All of this looking is too much for the future history teacher, being unpracticed at objective observation, so Tom escapes to his story books.

Mary, who was very curious about Dick, had gotten Tom to tell her all about his "potato-head" brother—about Tom's own attempt to teach him to read and about how their father had gotten angry at Tom and told him "don't learn him to read!" Mary and Tom felt sorry for Dick: "Young love. . . . How it wants to embrace everything, how sorry it feels for all those denied its simple remedy..." (*W*, 247). This feeling inspires them to enrich Dick's life by teaching him about love, and Mary agrees to begin his "sentimental education" (*W*, 248). After some instruction from Mary, Dick begins to ask questions of his father, Henry—questions like: Where do babies come from? Henry, in shocked response, answers that babies come from love. But Dick asks: "What's lu-love?" Henry replies: "Love, Dick is a feeling. A good feeling. It's like the feeling you felt for your poor Mum. Like the feeling she felt for you. . . . It's the most wonderful thing there is—" (*W*, 257). Thus Dick was, at the least, confused when Mary told him that her baby wasn't his and instead was Freddie's. What Dick was thinking nobody knows; and Tom, the observer-reporter-narrator, doesn't speculate about Dick's motive. There are, however, instances in which Dick appears to deceive Tom or to understand situations that were thought beyond his grasp.

After Mary's revelation, Tom, ever the historical sleuth, discovers an empty bottle of Coronation Ale that had floated up to the Atkinson Lock along with Freddie's body. Since there were two bruises on Freddie's head—only one of which was caused by Henry Crick's boathook when he fished Freddie out of the Leem—Tom concludes that the empty ale bottle was Dick's weapon. In order to confirm his suspicion, Tom baits Dick by placing the empty bottle where Dick will see it when he comes home from his dredging job and then locks his door when he hears Dick coming up the stairs. When Dick takes the bottle and hides it without saying anything or asking questions, Tom confirms that Mary was correct—Dick had killed Freddie.

After the coroner rules Freddie's death accidental, Tom cycles to the Hockwell Lode to tell Mary the good news. "It's all right," Tom tells Mary. "Haven't you heard? Accidental death. So it's all right. All right. Nothing's changed." Mary responds: "It's not all right. Because it wasn't an accident. Everything's changed" (*W*, 131).

Without Tom's knowing, Mary decides to force a miscarriage by jumping down off the windmill wall, and when they next meet at the Hockwell Lode, he finds her executing her plan. To no avail Tom pleads with her to stop. Finally, however, her jumping ceases.

"Something's happened," she says, looking up with the ghost of a laugh. "Works, after all."

Then she says, tears suddenly starting in her eyes: "Not Dick's. Ours. Ours. You understand?"

ᶜᵌ⁔

We crawl into the shell of the old windmill. Where once we sowed love, we wait for its precipitate fruit-fall. . . . Mary leans in my arms. She pulls up her skirt.

"Not much blood. Something's just happened inside. Just. Have to wait... See." (*W*, 294)

ᶜᵌ⁔

"Do you—understand?"

. . . I understand. Because if this baby had never... Then Dick would never... And Freddie... Because cause, effect... (*W*, 295)

Now, Mary and Tom have no choice: they must journey to Wash Fen Mere to seek the services of Martha Clay, a descendent of the marsh people who lived in the undrained, unreclaimed bogs and marshes of the Fens. Tom tries to explain to Martha why they've come to her, but

she says: "Oh, save it up, bor'! . . . You're a-goin to say that little missy
here's got somethin' she wants to get rid o'" (*W*, 302). Martha lives in a
Fen cottage full of old implements, pots and kettles; and hanging from
the ceilings are dead birds as well as "misshapen things blackened with
smoke that you don't ask what they are . . . [and] all manner of bags and
pouches that you don't like to ask what's inside" (*W*, 304). Tom recalls:
"we've . . . stepped into a different world. The one where things come to
a stop; the one where the past will go on happening" (*W*, 304). As a
result of that journey to Wash Fen Mere, Mary contracts an infection of
the womb and is taken to the hospital, where she almost dies. All
Hockwell knows the scandal:

> But only I know about that night in Martha's cottage. What I saw
> through the window. And that dawn. That dawn. I carried the pail, down
> to the Ouse. Because Martha said: "You gotta do it, bor. Only you. No one
> else. In the river, mind. An' when you throws it, don't you look. Nothin'
> but bad luck if you looks." So I carried the pail across the mist-wrapped,
> dew-soaked meadows. . . . I climbed the river wall, descended to the
> water's edge. I turned my head away. But then I looked. I howled. A
> farewell glance. A red spittle, floating, frothing, slowly sinking. Borne on
> the slow Ouse currents. Borne down-stream. Borne all the way (but for
> the Ouse eels...) to the Wash. Where it all comes out. (*W*, 316–17)

The virulence of this scandal, Tom believes, even penetrated "Dick's
duck's-back senses" (*W*, 316). When Dick leads Tom upstairs to his
room, he extracts a brass key from the mouth of the stuffed pike on his
wall—the one that Tom always feared as a little boy. Dick holds the key
out to Tom, a sign that Tom takes as confession that Dick killed Freddie.
Tom remembers:

> Something has got hold of him. Something as inescapable and inexplica-
> ble as the sudden grip of love. His face is aquiver with un-Dick-like
> importunacy. He wants releasing. He's got the key in his hand. For the
> first time in his life, the forgetful flux of Dick's experience has congealed
> around him into imprisoning solidity. He's as fixed as that pike on the
> wall. He's made things happen; things have happened because of him. He
> can't understand. He's stuck in the past. (*W*, 318)

Dick wants to understand what's happened and leads Tom into the
attic, where the black wooden chest, bequeathed to Dick by his mother
in 1937 on the night before she died of influenza, has been stored away.

The contents of the chest set Tom on his first true historical search. He reflects: "Once I toyed, once I dabbled in history. . . . But it never got serious—my studies never really began—until one August afternoon, a prisoner myself of irreversibly historical events, I unlocked the past inside a black wooden chest..." (*W*, 319–20).

> So I began to demand of history an Explanation. Only to uncover in this dedicated search more mysteries, more fantasticalities, more wonders and grounds for astonishment than I started with; only to conclude forty years later—notwithstanding a devotion to the usefulness, to the educative power of my chosen discipline—that history is a yarn. And can I deny that what I wanted all along was not some golden nugget that history would at last yield up, but History itself: the Grand Narrative, the filler of vacuums, the dispeller of fears of the dark? (*W*, 62)

Tom discovers that the chest—given to Dick by his mother, Helen—was actually bequeathed him by his grandfather Ernest Richard Atkinson. Inside the chest are ten bottles of a potent and legendary ale brewed by Helen and Ernest, along with one empty bottle, four notebooks, and a letter. Tom puts aside the notebooks, which he will later pore over in his search for an explanation, and picks up the three-page letter addressed to Dick as "First-Born of Mrs. Henry Crick" (*W*, 320). After silently reading the letter, he tries to explain its contents to Dick and that the letter is from their mother's father. Up to then, Tom had allowed Dick to believe that Mary's baby was Dick's. Then, almost inadvertently, he says: "Dick, I'm sorry. I lied to you. It wasn't your baby. It was my baby. . . . He stares at me. Because it's Dick's stare it's impossible to tell what he's thinking. But a sticky dew starts to collect in the corners of his eyes. Though it's not like tears. It's like some strange, unknown secretion that has nothing to do with Dick" (*W*, 321). In a series of attempts—"My father isn't your father." "Your mother was my mother." "You and your mother had the same father." (*W*, 322)—Tom tries to explain the incest between their mother and her father, including the mandate that Dick should never have children and the pronouncement by his grandfather-father that Dick would be the "Saviour of the World." Dick begins to wheeze, to gasp for air, and with each additional statement his wheeze hoarsens as if he is running out of air, like a fish out of water. Tom thinks that perhaps Dick understands, understands that he should never have been and that's there's been some kind of mix-up, for Dick says to him: "S-s-sorry, Tom. S-s-sorry"

(*W*, 323). Tom tries to calm Dick, telling him that he is "an unusual per-son," "a special sort of person." Tom muses to himself: "How can I put this into any other words? How can I preface, interpret, explain (your father was not only your grandfather, he must have been quite mad—): 'Because, Dick, you're going to be—you're going to be—the Saviour of the World'" (*W*, 323).

The next day, a Sunday, Dick avoids looking at the man he had always known as his dad and eventually goes off to the lean-to near the cottage, apparently to tinker with his motorcycle. Tom decides that he must tell his father everything—about Dick killing Freddie Parr, about the letter in the chest, and about Dick knowing that his grandfather was also his father. When Tom offers the letter to his father, Henry says: "I don't wanna see no letter, Tom. I never wanted to see inside that chest" (*W*, 325). And with tears in his eyes, Henry Crick "leaves his true-son standing and rushes, hobbles, towards his non-son's tempo-rary refuge, crying all the while: 'Dick—my poor Dick' (yes, *my* Dick) '—Dick!'" (*W*, 326), only to discover that Dick has left the lean-to. From the upper window, Tom sees Dick riding away with the chest, his "birthright on his back" (*W*, 327), and tells his dad that Dick is headed for the dredger, the *Rosa II*.

When Henry and Tom finally arrive at the Ouse they see Dick on the *Rosa II,* docked on the opposite bank. He is ostentatiously drinking ale from the chest. To no avail they shout for him to come back. Dick ignores them. By the time they are rowed out to the dredger, they hear the dredger start up,

> And with the sound, a smell also. The smell of something hauled from primitive depths. The smell that haunts Dick's bedroom.
> He's here. He knows his place. He knows his station. He keeps the lad-der turning, the buckets scooping. . . . And this smell of silt is the smell of sanctuary, is the smell of amnesia. He's here, he's now. Not there or then. No past, no future. . . .
> And he's the saviour of the world. (*W*, 355)

Henry shouts: "Dick, it's all right! Dick. I'll be your father..." (*W*, 356). Tom recalls the scene:

> But memory can't keep fixed and clear those final moments. Memory can't even be sure whether what I saw, I saw first in anticipation before I actually saw it, as if I had witnessed it somewhere already—a memory before it occurred. (*W*, 356)

Was it really the case (but how could I have been sure, in that fading light, at that bobbing distance?) that his eyelids were quite motionless and that his gaze, luminous and intent, ceased at a certain point to be aimed at us, but turned to contemplate the rippling, furling, vibrant surface of the Ouse? Did he move first or did I shout first? And did I really shout aloud, or did the words only ring in my brain (and echo ever after)?

"Dick—don't do it!" (*W*, 356)

For a moment he perches, poises, teeters on the rail, the dull glow of the western sky behind him. And then he plunges. In a long, reaching, powerful arc. Sufficiently long and reaching to quite discount the later theory that he must have become entangled in the anchor-chain or the sling-lines; sufficiently reaching and powerful for us to observe his body, in its flight through the air, form a single, taut and seemingly limbless continuum, so that an expert on diving might have judged that here indeed was a natural, here indeed was a fish of a man.

And punctures the water, with scarcely a splash. And is gone.

. . . He's on his way. Obeying instinct. Returning. The Ouse flows to the sea... (*W*, 357)

The novel—and the central story that launches Tom on his life of historical search for an explanation—ends in confusion over the sequence of seeing, shouting, diving, but also with an image: "On the bank in the thickening dusk, in the will-o'-the-wisp dusk, abandoned but vigilant, a motor-cycle" (*W*, 358). It is important that Tom describes the thickening dusk as the "will-o-the-wisp," for in the lore of the Fens the "will-o'-the-wisp" is an apparition that lures one on with deluded hope. And what was Tom's hope that by 1980, when the story is told to Tom's children, seems to him deluded?

In *Israel and Revelation*, volume I of *Order and History*, Voegelin stated in the preface: "The order of history emerges from the history of order." The last volume of *Order and History* he entitled *In Search of Order*. This volume was unfinished when he died, as was, inevitably, the human search of order. That he insisted on calling his last volume *In Search of Order* rather than *In Search for Order* acknowledged his discovery that experiences of order—of wonder, of the awe of existence—precede the conscious search of order and of disorder for the truth of existence. Moreover, he discovered in his search of order that human beings, from antiquity into the present, had experienced and symbolized

the order of reality as a community of being in which the partners—
God and man, world and society—"live the others' death/the others'
life die."

Tom Crick's historical search was no search *of* order, for Tom did not
believe that order (or meaning, as he calls it) exists. Or if it exists—as he
seems to think the divine exists—its existence is relevant, not to the lives
of mature human beings, but only to the lives of "backward peoples"
and children, to assuage their fears. Nor was Tom's search a search *for*
order; it was a search for an explanation rooted in the question "when
did things go wrong?" This question entailed the recognition that things
did not go wrong just when he and Mary began exploring "holes and
things," but that . . .

there had been Freddie putting a live eel down Mary's knickers,
there had been his father Henry saying, years earlier, that God with-
holds his blessings from humans because we are wicked,
there had been, before that, the "potato-head" product of Helen
Crick and her father, intended as "the saviour of the world,"
there had been the long-unresolved historical controversy "about
the still obscure life cycle of this snake-like, fish-like, highly edible, not
to say phallically suggestive creature" (*W,* 196) *Anguilla anguilla,* the
European eel,
there had been the prophetic, ghostly figure of the Atkinson ancestor
Sara, who had withdrawn from society following a beating at the hands
of her husband in the 1700s, but who is ever present in the superstitions
of the fens.

Although Tom's historical curiosity over "when things went wrong"
is overwhelming, he never asks: Where did it all come from? Where did
we come from? Where did I come from? Tom's search traps him—for
the "why" that Tom attributes to the animal man is a "why" that relies
upon the time-bound model of cause and effect. Even as he spars with
the school's headmaster, a scientist, Tom is trapped by his epistemology—the misunderstood epistemology of modern natural science and
its untenable misapplication to human history.

So I began to look into history—not only the well-thumbed history of
the wide world but also, indeed with particular zeal, the history of my
Fenland forebears. So I began to demand of history an Explanation.
Only to uncover in this dedicated search more mysteries, more

fantasticalities, more wonders and grounds for astonishment than I started with; only to conclude forty years later—notwithstanding a devotion to the usefulness, to the educative power of my chosen discipline—that history is a yarn. And can I deny that what I wanted all along was not some golden nugget that history would at last yield up, but History itself: the Grand Narrative, the filler of vacuums, the dispeller of fears of the dark? (*W*, 62)

Tom's student Price exposes Tom's talk of Explanation. Price says to Tom in an after-school detention conference: "explaining's a way of avoiding the facts while you pretend to get near to them ... [T]he more explaining you hear, the more you think things must be pretty bad that they need so much explaining" (*W*, 167). Tom soon concludes instead that history must be a yarn, but "so long as we have this itch for explanations, must we not always carry round with us this cumbersome but precious bag of clues called History?" (*W*, 10). Tom doesn't pursue his search into the myth of the time of the creation, for he sees the myth only as a source for retrieving the facts of history with "empirical fishing lines."

> There are times when we have to disentangle history from fairy-tale. There are times (they come round really quite often) when good dry textbook history takes a plunge into the old swamps of myth and has to be retrieved with empirical fishing lines. History, being an accredited sub-science, only wants to know the facts. History, if it is to keep on constructing its road into the future, must do so on solid ground. At all costs let us avoid mystery-making and speculation, secrets and idle gossip. And, for God's sake, nothing supernatural. And above all, let us not tell *stories*. (*W*, 86)

As we have seen in Voegelin's case, the experience of disorder, of things going wrong, as a stimulus for the philosophical search is balanced with an experience of wonder, of the awe of existence. In fact Tom's search reveals "more mysteries, more fantasticalities, more wonders and grounds for astonishment" (*W*, 62) than he had started with. But for Tom, the search for the beginning remains a single-minded search in time for the "time" when "things" went wrong.

The contraction of Tom's mind to wrongness rooted in "time" and "things" dates to a "time" several months after the death of his mother:

> When the [eel] traps were set we lay back on the river-bank. ... Up above, the sky swarmed with stars which seemed to multiply as we looked at

them. And as we lay, Dad said: "Do you know what the stars are? They are the silver dust of God's blessing. They are little broken-off bits of heaven. God cast them down to fall on us. But when he saw how wicked we were, he changed his mind and ordered the stars to stop." (*W*, 1–2)

What we witness in *Waterland* is a quest that excludes the crucial questions, a quest limited even before it began, because the divine partner in the community of Being was banished from Tom's youthful consciousness. What he remembers could have been a moment of awe and wonder in his young life, but instead he remembers only that the stars—"the silver dust of God's blessing"—are withheld from man. Even though Tom understood that God was ever present and watching over the Fens, since He had a clear and unobstructed view, God was not experienced by Tom as a participant in his life, either as a child or as an adult. Tom's and Mary's actions—leading to the deaths of three people—confirmed for Tom his father's pronouncement that humans are wicked.

Mary, on the other hand, recognizes, at some level, her need for the divine. Her actions during the three years following the abortion suggest contrition and penance; but her curiosity was gone, and she had become indifferent to life. Tom wonders "whether the truth of those three years was that nothing, nothing at all, occurred and that the future Mrs. Crick, gazing day after day from her farmhouse cell at the level fields, was only, wittingly or unwittingly, preparing herself for her later marriage—which would be a sort of fenland" (*W*, 118).

At the age of fifty-three (the narrative present), Mary actively seeks the divine. She admits to Tom that she has been talking to a priest and has been to confession for the first time in almost forty years. Tom is appalled by the books—*If Jesus Returned; God, or The Bomb*—that she brings home to read. Since the reader is not privy to Mary's search (because Tom is not privy), we know little about it. We only know that Tom cannot credit her search as genuine. We know also that Mary became obsessed with having a child that God promised to send; for since the abortion, as Mary had told Tom in 1944, "short of a miracle" she could not have a child (*W*, 122). We know that she stole a child because she believed God had told her to do so. And we realize that without the divine presence in her life, Mary cannot overcome the indifference that was born as her curiosity died at the old windmill on Hockwell Lode. Her curiosity, which died with the love it had begotten, had first joined her to and then separated her from her love of the world. When she resumes her search for the divine in 1980, it prompts the modern response: she is placed in a mental hospital. Tom the historian knows enough to comment: "In another age . . . they might have called her holy (or else have burnt her as a witch). . . . They might have allowed her the full scope of her mania: her anchorite's cell, her ascetic's liberties, her visions and ravings..." (*W*, 330).

Tom's double diagnosis of Mary and her judges belies his recognition of the In-Between reality—the *metaxy*—of human existence. From the beginning, he recognizes all the members of the community of being—God and man, world and society. But even though the human and cosmic junctures of the Time of the Tale echo through his search for an explanation, the divine element manifests itself in strange, bizarre, and deformed ways; it is permitted only to children, to ghosts, and to "primitives."

As Tom struggles with an explanation for Mary's theft of the baby, he asks, "How? Why? Why?"; and when she responds, "God told me. God...," he reflects:

> But God doesn't talk any more. Didn't you know that, Mary? He stopped talking long ago. He doesn't even watch any more, up there in the sky. We've grown up now, and we don't need him any more, our Father in Heaven. We can fend for ourselves. He's left us alone to make what we will of the world. . . . God's for simple, backward people in God-forsaken places. (*W*, 268)

Just as Mary's knowledge that she cannot "fend for" herself results in her quest for the divine, Tom's search, structured by his quest for a beginning in time when things went wrong, runs up against the mystery of a cosmic beginning—the search for the mysterious creational beginning of the life cycle of the eel that he includes in the final version of the Tale he tells his students—his children. "Curiosity," Tom lectures his students,

> will never be content. Even today, when we know so much, curiosity has not unraveled the riddle of the birth and sex life of the eel. Perhaps these are things, like many others, destined never to be learnt before the world comes to its end. Or perhaps—but here I speculate, here my own curiosity leads me by the nose—the world is so arranged that when all things are learnt, when curiosity is exhausted (so, long live curiosity), that is when the world shall have come to its end. (*W*, 204)

This reflection suggests that at some level Tom has realized that a search for the Beginning is also a search for the Beyond, a search of order writ large. But just as he roots wrongness in time and things, Tom searches, not for the beginning of the eel as a synecdoche for creation, the Beginning, but only for what scientists know about it; he searches "natural history" for the facts of the origin of *Anguilla anguilla*. Even though he declares that there are things that humans cannot learn before the "world comes to its end," does he understand the implications of his declaration? Would not the end of the world signify the end of humanity, and who then would "know" these "things"? In this almost unconscious insight, undeveloped and consciously unexplored as it is, we dimly perceive Tom's recognition of the mystery of Being, the mystery of the Beginning and the Beyond. Thus even as Tom experiences the cosmos with its beginning and lastingness as "the habitat of man,"[4] he cannot engage in a search of the beginning; for to him creation is only a myth, a fabulation, a fairy-tale told to calm the fears of the Fenspeople. "When did things go wrong?" is the wrong question and issues not in an inconclusive quest but in a barren one. Tom suspends his story, and his barren quest, after Mary is locked away.

> He sits up all night. Reads. Smokes. Works his way down a whisky bottle. Marks essays and piles of notes (the last harvestings of thirty-two years). Drunken red-ink scrawls. . . . To comfort himself he tells himself stories. He repeats the stories he's told his class. Ah, the contrast of these hollow nights and his well-thronged days: classroom chatter, playground bedlam...But not long now before even they—
>
> ∽
>
> We all wander from the real world, we all come to our asylums. (*W,* 331)

Tom's asylum is the past. The present is disappearing from his life, and this present—his students—was in Tom's mind the only future available to him; but what he had believed to be his real future was aborted long ago, back in 1943 when he dumped the fetal contents of the pail—"In the pail is what the future's made of" (*W,* 308), he recalls—into the Great River Ouse. The future Tom now faces contains only reading (what does Tom read? I wonder), smoking, drinking, and the feeble attempt to comfort himself with his past, with the stories he told his students.

Only the past remains, and the content of the past that Tom remembers in order to comfort himself is the stories he told his children. But

---

4. Voegelin, "The Beginning and the Beyond," 177.

the stories do not comfort him; these nights of reading, smoking, booz-
ing are "hollow nights" contrasted with his last days in the classroom. In
days to come, Tom will mark time in his own asylum.

5

# "A Secret between Man and God"

### Second Reality in Heimito von Doderer's
### *The Demons*

The public life of society is . . . characterized not only by the spirit, but also through the possibility of estrangement from it.

~ ERIC VOEGELIN,
"THE GERMAN UNIVERSITY AND THE ORDER OF GERMAN SOCIETY:
A RECONSIDERATION OF THE NAZI ERA"

Terrible things took place in my native land and in this, my native city, at a time long after the grave and lighthearted stories I wish to relate here had come to an end. And one thing that lay curled amorphous and germinal within the events that I must recount, emerged dripping blood, took on a name, became visible to the eye which had been almost blinded by the vortex of events, shot forth, and was, even in its beginnings, recognizable—gruesomely inconspicuous and yet distinctly recognizable for what it was.

~ HEIMITO VON DODERER. "OVERTURE," *THE DEMONS*

---

I n this chapter I explore Doderer's symbolization of "second reality" as it is developed in his novel *The Demons*.[1] Since Voegelin adopted the term *second reality* from Robert Musil and *Apperzeptions-*

---

1. Since the German edition is entitled *Die Dämonen: Nach der Chronik des Sektionsrates Geyrenhoff* (Munich: Biederstein Verlag, 1956), the full English title would be *The Demons: After the Chronicle by the Department Councillor Geyrenhoff.*

*Verweigerung* from Doderer, who also uses the term *second reality,* the first section of the chapter discusses Voegelin's understanding and use of these symbols. The second part "summarizes" *The Demons,* while the third section raises interpretive difficulties with specific attention to Doderer's use of a passage from Tacitus for the epigraph to the novel. Part four presents a general overview of Doderer's depiction of characters living in second reality; the fifth part focuses on the narrator-chronicler Georg von Geyrenhoff's Hobbyhorse Chronicle of *Die Unsrigen;* and the final section includes general concluding observations.

## SECOND REALITY IN VOEGELIN'S PHILOSOPHY

For Voegelin, the importance of the works of the Germanic novelists and playwrights—like Elias Canetti (Austrian), Doderer (Austrian), Friedrich Dürrenmatt (Swiss), Max Frisch (Swiss), Thomas Mann (German), and Robert Musil (Austrian)—lies in their exploration of estrangement from the spiritual substance of reality as comprehensively constituted by God and man, world and society, as partners in the community of being. The imaginative constructions of second reality (Hegel, for example, or Schlaggenberg in *The Demons*) that emerge from this estrangement and issue in ideological systems are rooted in a misunderstanding of human imagination as an autonomous capacity of man to create symbolic language. Primarily, Voegelin identifies the second reality with ideological systems imaginatively constructed in resistance to, or rejection of, the divine component in the quaternarian structure of reality. Addressing the "literary response" to Germany's spiritual disorientation in his essay on the German university, he writes:

When the first reality, which is the expression of spiritual substance, cannot be developed because of the absence of such substance, in its place there will develop an artificial reality—that is, a reality that has the external form of reality but which is not substantially supported by the spirit. We enter here upon a realm of spiritlike nonspirit or anti-spirit, which finds its representation on the plane of politics in the ideological mass movements. Doderer in particular, in his book *The Demons,* has been concerned with the second reality as a phenomenon of social and political disorder. Doderer has furthermore located the origin of the second reality in the refusal of apperception. The "world view" as a characteristic case of second reality he defines as "a refusal of apperception elevated to a system." When the refusal to apperceive [*Apperzeptions-Verweigerung*] becomes radical, it leads to the phenomenon of total self- and world-annihilation, which Doderer has treated in the grotesque of his *Merowinger.*[2]

In the essay "On Debate and Existence," Voegelin defined the "untruth of existence as a revolt against the *condicio humana* and the attempt to overlay its reality by the construction of a Second Reality."[3] And in his essay "On Hegel: A Study in Sorcery," Voegelin analyzes the elaborate lengths to which Hegel went to construct his Second Reality so that it was obliquely related to the First and Actual Reality:

> In order to be effective as a magic opus, the System of Science had to satisfy two conditions:
> 1. The operation in Second Reality had to look as if it were an operation in First Reality.
> 2. The operation in Second Reality had to escape control and judgment by the criteria of First Reality.
> Only if he satisfied these two conditions, could the author of the system hope to make the imaginary results of his operation acceptable as real resolutions to real problems in the First Reality.[4]

Voegelin says that "the spiritual disease" of *Apperzeptions-Verweigerung* represents a closure to the various dimensions of, and a refusal to live consciously in openness to, reality, which manifests itself in the experience of "existential tension toward the ground" of being. When a person

> rebels against the ground, refusing to participate in reality and thus to experience his own reality as man, it is not the "world" that is thereby changed; instead it is he who loses contact with reality and suffers a loss of reality content in regard to his own person. Yet on this account he does not cease to be a man; and since his consciousness continues to intend a form of reality, he will generate substitute images of reality in order to gain order and direction for his existence and actions in the world. Consequently, he lives in a "second reality," as this phenomenon is called since Musil's *Der Mann ohne Eigenschaften.* The substitute images can draw their reality contents from various sources, the most important ones being the lust for wealth, power, or sex, as well as the *superbia vitae,* positing the autonomous Ego in place of the ground of being. The loss of reality results in pneumopathological disturbances in the existential

2. Voegelin, "The German University and the Order of German Society: A Reconsideration of the Nazi Era," 16.
   3. Voegelin, "On Debate and Existence," 49.
   4. Voegelin, "On Hegel: A Study in Sorcery," 242.

order of the respective person, and if life in the "second reality" becomes socially dominant, there follow the massive disturbances of social order with which we are all too familiar.[5]

Finally, Voegelin argues that it is impossible to know what induces an individual to revolt against reality by constructing an imaginary second reality. About Hegel, he asks

> What induced a potential philosopher to go on the rampage of becoming the Great-Great Man is impenetrable. As in the case of Hegel's great successors in sorcery, of Marx and Nietzsche who wanted to evoke the *Übermensch*, the spiritual disease of refusing to apperceive reality, and of closing one's existence through the construction of an imaginary Second Reality, is a secret between man and God. One can do no more than describe the phenomenon.[6]

Doderer's novelistic exploration and symbolization of second reality includes not only a description of the existential mode of living in a second reality but also an exploration of the genesis of, as well as the extrication from, the second reality. Influenced by Albert Gütersloh, Doderer intended *The Demons* to be a total novel. A total novel does not have a central theme; instead it aims to portray, painstakingly and accurately, the individual lives of characters and their relationships, as well as the interactions between an individual character and the external environment—both social and material—in which a character finds himself. Elizabeth Hesson observes that *The Demons* is unified, nonetheless, by the primary theme of second reality.[7]

### THE DEMONS: AN OVERVIEW

While *The Demons* has several plot lines, the main one deals with the accidental discovery by the first-person narrator, Georg von Geyrenhoff, of an attempt by Financial Counselor Levielle to defraud Charlotte von Schlaggenberg (called "Quapp") of her financial inheritance, which is clouded by the mystery of her parentage. At the time of the discovery, Geyrenhoff was chronicling the activities of *die Unsrigen,* a loosely organized group of various individual types living and socializing

5. Voegelin, *Anamnesis,* 368–69.
6. Voegelin, "On Hegel," 232.
7. Hesson, *Twentieth Century Odyssey: a Study of Heimito von Doderer's* Die Dämonen, 13.

in Vienna from November 1926 through the spring of 1927. After his discovery of the fraud attempt, Geyrenhoff stops writing the chronicle and
becomes involved in trying to recover Quapp's inheritance for her. In
part, his actions that involve the life and affairs of Quapp lead him to an
involvement with Friederike Ruthmayr, the widow of Quapp's real father,
Captain Georg Ruthmayr, and to his emergence from the second reality
he had indulged in by his obsessive chronicling. This main plot line is
embedded in and told against the backdrop of the activities of *die
Unsrigen*. Geyrenhoff's chronicling activities ultimately lead him to question his own biographical veracity, as he realizes that his psychic condition and the unrealistic expectation that he could chronicle all the lives
of *die Unsrigen* in fact cause him to overlook crucial realities. On the
other hand, the chronicling also plays a role in leading him back into the
first reality.

Other plot lines involve revolutionary activities in the Burgenland;
the educational development and maturation of the worker Leon
Kakabsa; the medieval story of a baron's deviant sexual obsession and
its inheritance by a contemporary businessman, Jan Herzka; the story of
a criminal named Meisgeier (the "Claw"); and the personal story lines
of members of *die Unsrigen*—Quapp's attempts to become a professional violinist, Quapp's love life, Kajetan von Schlaggenberg's sexual
obsession, René von Stangeler's career and love life, the relationship
between an American lepidopterist and a Prague stenographer, and the
events leading to the burning of the Palace of Justice on July 15, 1927.[8]
The penultimate long and brilliant chapter, "Das Feuer," weaves
together most of the story lines and characters of the novel and their
activities on the day the Palace of Justice is burned. While I have alluded
to several of the subplot lines to suggest the complexity of the novel, I
will not attempt to summarize them.[9]

8. The Palace of Justice was burned on July 15, 1927, by communists who rejected
the lenient judgment of the court on fascists who had shot and killed an old World War
I veteran and a young boy participating in a communist march in Schattendorf. By
Geyrenhoff's account in the chapter "Das Feuer," certain criminal elements like
Meisgeier, the "Claw," exacerbated the violence of the situation.

9. Most of the plot lines and characters are united by the theme of second reality.
Those characters who do not live in a second reality are, however, important as touchstones for those who do. Since most of the characters of the novel are living in some sort
of second reality, it would take a comprehensive description and analysis of the nature
of each character's second reality, as well as the relation of each character living in a second reality to a character living in the first reality, to fully appreciate the nature of second reality and life as Doderer understood them. Neither time nor space permits such
an extensive survey-analysis. The reader is advised to read through appendix 4 herein
before proceeding.

## The Demons: Complexity and Problems of Interpretation

There is no more apt, if unintended, description of *The Demons* than novelist and critic Milan Kundera's assertion that "the novel's spirit is the spirit of complexity. Every novel says to the reader: 'Things are not as simple as you think.' That is the novel's eternal truth."[10] The complexity of *The Demons* is manifest in several ways—in form, in substance, and in the biographical influences of the author's life. As we have noted, Doderer intended to write a "total novel" that aimed at "portraying 'the totality of life.'" This commitment resulted in a lengthy narrative—1,329 pages in the English edition and 1,344 in the German—that includes more than 140 characters.[11] Many of these characters appear not only in subplot lines but also in the main plot line, woven into various types of relationships with the principal characters of the central plot. So the first level of complexity that confronts the reader is the density of the plot itself, which is surpassed by very few modern novels. Doderer's own contention that "a work of narrative art is all the more legitimate the less a summary of contents will give us an idea of it" conveys a sense of the difficulties involved.[12]

To the complexity that the total novel carries within its plots (i.e., the extreme length and the large number of characters) must be added the problem of narration itself. Geyrenhoff, the first-person narrator, purports to write a chronicle of *die Unsrigen*, yet in the course of the novel he becomes more than the observer-chronicler he intended originally to be; he becomes one of the characters of his own chronicle and is supplanted eventually by the omniscient narrator he discovers himself not to be.[13] The nature of the chronicle intended by Geyrenhoff adds to the complexity:

---

10. Kundera, "Depreciated Legacy of Cervantes," 18.

11. Cf. List of Characters supplied by the translators of *The Demons*, English edition, 1330–34.

12. Doderer, *Repertorium*, 72. Quoted in Bachem, *Heimito von Doderer*, 83.

13. The exact point in terms of the chronology of events when this "replacement" occurs cannot be easily determined, since Geyrenhoff speaks throughout the narrative and since the omniscient narrator intrudes early as well as late in the novel. At the dead center of the German edition (p. 669; p. 684 of the English edition) we read: "But in von Geyrenhoff's case good intentions had always been more in evidence than any capacity for clear thinking. For that very reason only relatively small parts of his 'Chronicle' or whatever it was supposed to be, have been included in these pages. He himself, incidentally, always intended to make the 'final revision' of all the reports himself, but of course that was altogether out of the question. He did not revise; he was revised." In theory, it

> My occupation was nothing more nor less than to keep a diary for a
> whole group of persons, principally those whom I shall later refer to as
> "our crowd." It was, however, not only the diary of a collective entity—as
> a ship's log might be, or the account of an expedition among savage
> tribes. Rather, I conscientiously performed my task for each individual of
> the group and kept my eye on him constantly. (*Ds*, 6)

Since Geyrenhoff's original project, as intended, would have compelled
him to be everywhere, seeing and hearing everything that everyone said,
he obviously required additional sources of information. In fact, he
asserts early in the novel that his sources include—in addition to notes
written up by him "immediately after the event"—willing contributors,
who either wrote narratives themselves or reported to Geyrenhoff on
events of the group that he had missed, and unwitting collaborators
whom Geyrenhoff sounded out. His dreams, which as he indicates are
"really no longer dreams but rather insights," become an additional
source upon which he depends for his chronicle (*Ds*, 13). More important, it is this source, "dreams as insights," that permits Geyrenhoff to
understand that his chronicling was part of the complex of occurrences
and activities that led to his emergence from second reality. The information gathered from the sources by Geyrenhoff is included in the
novel in various ways and with varying degrees of attribution. Some of
the information appears in the form of edited manuscripts (the
*Chronique Scandaleuse*), some in the form of entire "historical" manuscripts (like the medieval manuscript discovered in the library at Castle
Neudegk), and some without any attribution, even though it is obvious
in such cases that Geyrenhoff himself is not the source. Although
Geyrenhoff in the beginning claims the advantage of hindsight, he
maintains that his "facial expression . . . must not be painted as more
knowing than it was at the time in question" (*Ds*, 7).

The narrative's construction with respect to time offers another
dimension of complexity. First, the events of the novel are not told
chronologically. The reader must carefully construct a time line of
events in order to understand exactly what happened and when.[14] The
stories that Geyrenhoff tells take place between autumn 1926 and July

---

should be possible to determine which of the two narrators is speaking in passages
where the name Geyrenhoff appears, for in the German edition the narrator Geyrenhoff
refers to himself as "G——ff." Thus, whenever a passage in the German edition spells out
the name Geyrenhoff, the omniscient narrator is speaking. The English translators
spelled out Geyrenhoff in both instances. See translators' note to English edition.

14. See appendix 5.

18, 1927, approximately ten months. The narrator clearly states that he
began recording the story during the events he describes but that he put
the chronicle down before the numerous stories worked themselves out,
only to pick up the various notes, chronicles, and manuscripts again in
1955. This style of writing a story, i.e., of starting to write, collecting
notes, putting aside the writing and notes only to take them up and
complete the story much later, parallels the writing of a story told by
Ruodlieb van der Vläntsch, whose manuscript of 1517 was provided by
Stangeler and interpolated into the novel by Geyrenhoff. The actual
events described in Ruodlieb's manuscript occurred in 1464, fifty-three
years before the story was written down. The mode of telling the story
of the novel and the interpolated manuscript of Ruodlieb van der
Vläntsch, in turn, parallel Doderer's own process of writing *The Demons*.
He began writing the novel in 1929, shortly after its principal historical
event—the burning of the Palace of Justice on July 15, 1927—and wrote
until 1936. In 1936, he imposed upon himself a period of gestation.
This period, which he called *Gedächtnis-Distanz,* continued until April
1951, when Doderer began writing the novel again. It was finished in
July 1956, twenty-seven years after he had begun. The period of
*Gedächtnis-Distanz* was necessary because Doderer had reached an
impasse in the obsessive narrative of the novel's obsessive characters.
This brings us to another complexity of the novel, rooted in Doderer's
own life: the narrative problems that his private and public past created
in the writing. Ultimately, these problems call into question the veracity of the story and, thereby, the veracity of its author. Doderer's selec-
tion of a passage from the *Histories* of Tacitus as an epigraph to the
novel suggests an awareness of this essentially autobiographical problem, a problem of his own historical entanglement with the plot and its
narration. In Latin, this epigraph reads: "malignitati falsa species libertatis inest" (malignity makes a false show of independence).[15]

The difficulties inherent in isolating independence from malignity
are inscribed in Doderer's own life story. Doderer studied history and
psychology at the University of Vienna (1920–1927), received his doctorate in history (1925), and later studied at the Institute for Austrian
Historical Research (1946–1950). The professions of two of Doderer's
primary characters—Kajetan von Schlaggenberg, a novelist, and René
von Stangeler, a historian—mirror the training and activities of
Doderer. From 1931 to 1938, he was a member of the illegal (in Austria)

---

15. Tacitus, *The Histories,* 3.

National Socialist party, from which he resigned after the Anschluss, converting shortly thereafter to Roman Catholicism. Because he had been a member of the National Socialist party, he was not able to publish under his own name for several years after World War II. During this time he published under the *nom de plume* Stangeler. A third primary character who mirrors Doderer's life is the narrator Geyrenhoff, who, while not an overt fascist, is closely related to and associated with fascists in the novel, notably his nephew Kurt Körger. In 1929 Doderer began writing *Die Dämonen der Ostmark* but reached an impasse in his writing in 1936 and, as noted above, did not work on the novel from 1936 to 1951, when he began writing again. He finished the novel, which had by now been renamed *Die Dämonen: Nach der Chronik des Sektionsrates Geyrenhoff* (*The Demons: After the Chronicle by the Department Councillor Geyrenhoff*), in July 1956.

With these aspects of Doderer's biography in mind, we ask: Can we believe what the author has revealed to us about the experience of living in second reality? On the one hand, common sense assumes that a writer writes from within his own experience. Yet because National Socialism not only was an ideological system that denied and rejected the community of human beings but was also thoroughly defeated militarily, we at least have to consider the possibility that the novel may simply elaborate a carefully calculated rationalization designed to redeem the unsavory components of Doderer's past. Could Doderer have been attempting to excuse his Nazi past—claiming possession by demons even—rather than assuming responsibility for his own history?

In order to address these questions, I will reflect briefly on the passage from Tacitus from which the epigraph ("malignitati falsa species libertatis inest") was drawn. The whole sentence in which the epigraph appears reads: "But while men quickly turn from a historian who curries favour, they listen with ready ears to calumny and spite; for flattery is subject to the shameful charge of servility, but malignity makes a false show of independence."[16] Tacitus maintains that readers are repulsed by flattery and its overtones of servility, but are persuaded, falsely, of the truth of a malevolent chronicle.[17] A novelist who is a former Nazi does seem to face a dilemma, especially if he chooses to write about that aspect of his past.

16. Ibid., 3. The Latin reads: "Sed ambitionem scriptoris facile averseris, obtrectatio et livor pronis auribus accipiuntur; quippe adulationi foedum crimen servitutis, malignitati falsa species libertatis inest."
17. The English translators render the epigraph as "Malevolence wears the false face of honesty."

Does the epigraph from Tacitus point to the dimensions of this dilemma or does it simply provide Doderer with what Voegelin calls an "alibi" that permits an unauthentic "mastery of the past"?[18]

The larger context of the passage may provide clues to Doderer's use of Tacitus for the epigraph:

> Many historians have treated the earlier period of eight hundred and twenty years from the founding of Rome, and while dealing with the Republic they have written with equal eloquence and freedom. But after the battle of Actium, when the interests of peace required that all power should be concentrated in the hands of one man, writers of like ability disappeared; and at the same time historical truth was impaired in many ways: first, because men were ignorant of politics as being not any concern of theirs; later, because of their passionate desire to flatter; or again, because of their hatred of their masters. So between the hostility of the one class and the servility of the other, posterity was disregarded. But while men quickly turn from a historian who curries favour, they listen with ready ears to calumny and spite; for flattery is subject to the shameful charge of servility, but malignity makes a false show of independence.[19]

After the naval battle fought at Actium,[20] when a dictatorship was deemed necessary, the disappearance of eloquent and independent

18. As one might expect, the passage from Tacitus opens numerous points of contact between *The Demons* and Voegelin's analysis of *Hitler and the Germans*. The term *alibi*, which Voegelin finds in Karl Kraus, refers to a strand of National Socialist propaganda according to which "the uncommitted theft" provides the "alibi for the thousand murders" (91). Under this aspect, Doderer's posture toward his past, abjuring the poles of flattery and malevolence, might lead the reader to suspect an "alibi." Voegelin's critique of German historiography of Hitler, which had inclined toward "excluding all that is relevant" (55), including the Germans themselves, proceeds through a discussion of "The Cliché of the 'Unmastered Past'" (70). As Voegelin suggests, it is the present that one must master, in full recognition of an unmasterable divine Presence. Doderer's Geyrenhoff, the revising and revised storyteller, will confront all of these problems.

19. Tacitus, *Histories*, 3. The Latin reads: "Nam post conditam urbem octingentos et viginti prioris aevi annos multi auctores rettulerunt, dum res populi Romani memorabantur pari eloquentia ac libertate: postquam bellatum apud Actium atque omnem potentiam ad unum conferri pacis interfuit, magna illa ingenia cessere; simul veritas pluribus modis infracta, primum inscitia rei publicae ut alienae, mox libidine adsentandi aut rursus odio adversus dominantis. Ita neutris cura posteritatis inter infensos vel obnoxios. Sed ambitionem scriptoris facile averseris, obtrectatio et livor pronis auribus accipiuntur; quippe adulationi foedum crimen servitutis, malignitati falsa species libertatis inest (ibid., 2).

20. In this battle, fought in 31 BC, the forces of Octavian under Agrippa defeated the sea and land forces of Antony and Cleopatra and established Octavian as ruler of Rome. The rule of Augustus, Octavian, became wholly constitutional only in January, 27 BC. Cf. Tacitus, *Histories*, 2, n 3.

historians threatened "historical truth." Writers became uninterested in
politics; then they either indulged their passion to flatter their masters,
thus distorting "historical truth," or so hated their masters that they dis-
torted "historical truth" in another direction. To this recipe for the
betrayal of posterity must be added, by implication, the failure to attend
to public affairs, which leads to the bare choice between flattery and
malice, with the latter indulging readers' weakness for a chronicle
tinged with such ill will. If this is a fair reading of Tacitus, we may postulate that Doderer is also asserting that a writer's responsibility
requires a concern for politics in its original sense.

By his choice of this epigraph, might not Doderer be saying, "If I
malign this period that I am chronicling, it will be a false show of independence from it"? If this reading is accurate, Doderer may further be
saying that he cannot divorce himself from this period of his life in
order to understand it; he cannot describe his previous life in a second
reality in a posture of malice or detachment, no matter how favorably
his malice would be received by readers. Nor can he abdicate his responsibility as a writer to posterity by abandoning politics as though it had
nothing to do with him. What is left to Doderer? He must avoid servility to his past; he must avoid hatred of his past; he must embrace the
writer's (historian-novelist's) responsibility to posterity with the same
commitment as the writers of the Roman Republic, i.e., with eloquence
and freedom. Yet, we must still ask: Can an account of second reality as
a mode of existence written by a former Nazi be credited? Is Doderer's
epigraph obliquely requesting this of his reader? Or does this epigraph
suggest, finally, that he is willing to forego the "ready ears" of readers
attracted to the false liberty implied by a malicious story, in hopes of
honoring posterity?

## LIFE (OR ACTUAL REALITY), SECOND REALITY, AND *APPERZEPTIONS-VERWEIGERUNG*

People who wished to see the rigid concrete channels of their lives extended
into the infinite future were in fact doing nothing but stalling the continual
delicate vacillations of reality. And the moment that vibrant equilibrium was
halted, a second reality came into being: the rigid, isolated second reality of
. . . Lord Achaz, and of all those others who knew precisely how things should
be and whom they ought to shoot at, and why.

~ RENÉ VON STANGELER, HISTORIAN

In order to understand Doderer's formulation of second reality and the importance that *Apperzeptions-Verweigerung* plays in that formulation, it is necessary to describe very briefly what he calls the first or actual reality. This first reality is simply life—or the human condition—as human beings experience it and the openness of life to "the continual delicate vacillations of reality." Life as it presents itself for our experience must be distinguished from the abstraction Life. As human beings, using our mortal reason, we cannot make sense of the abstraction Life; we cannot discern an abstract pattern of meaning that transcends the individual occurrences of our lives. Consequently, we cannot discern in history an abstract or total pattern of meaning. We must simply face and accept life as it comes to us. Accepting life as it presents itself involves apperception, the conscious recognition and understanding of perception.

One of Doderer's alter egos, the novelist Schlaggenberg, attempts to formulate the problem of apperception and consciousness metaphorically. "Every real apperception," he says, "is not only a contact and superficial mingling of inner and outer; it is an interpenetration of both—more than that, a chemical process, a compound, an 'alchemical marriage' between us and the world, in which we are playing the feminine role" (*Ds*, 1076–77). After he has ended his chronicling and while he is attempting to protect Quapp's inheritance, Geyrenhoff uses a different metaphor: "every man has a number of electrical outlets within him. Some of them may never be plugged in, but the means for conducting a current exists, even though that current may come from a veritable hereafter in the here. What is intelligence but conductivity, readiness to let currents flow?" (*Ds*, 1148).

These metaphors—the alchemical-sexual and the electrical—represent characters' efforts to configure the way in which the world (life, or first reality) registers in an individual consciousness. The alchemical dimension of the alchemical-sexual metaphor essentially presents a picture of consciousness as a mixing of the inner and outer worlds; apperception in this image is like a chemical compound created through chemical reaction. The sexual dimension of the metaphor assigns to human beings the feminine role in sexual intercourse, while the outer world (the first reality) assumes the male role. If penetration fails, there is no apperception, no sexual experience. The electrical metaphor, on the other hand, presents human intelligence as a number of electrical outlets, which may or may not be connected to an energy source; if the outlet is plugged into an energy source, the electrical current may flow and apperception may be experienced. These metaphors assume the existence and interpenetration of two entities: inner world/outer world; female/male; electrical wiring/electrical current. They are less precise concerning the condition of openness to the "continual delicate vacillations of reality" (*Ds*, 1237) that is necessary to maintain the "vibrant equilibrium" that characterizes apperception. Both metaphors symbolize the capacity for experience and apperception as well as the capacity for refusal of apperception, or *Apperzeptions-Verweigerung*. Only by remaining open to the "continual delicate vacillations" does the human being exist in the present and in tension with his partners in the community of being and thereby maintain the truth of his existence in the *metaxy*. In order for apperception to occur, the dualities must become unities: what is really out there must be permitted fully to appear in consciousness. Confronted with life's variety, the human being is free to choose to apprehend or to refuse to apprehend. If the outlets are blocked, a conscious choice, then the electrical current cannot flow.

*The Demons* presents several characters who are living in the first (and actual) reality. Kyrill Scolander, an artist-novelist and Schlaggenberg's teacher, and Mary K., a widow who has lost her leg in a tram accident, are touchstones for some of the characters who live in second reality. Scolander lives fully in reality and is characterized as exactly opposite to someone who is living in second reality. In fact, the narrator calls Scolander a Pythia, the title of the priestess of the Delphic Oracle; of course, the Oracle at Delphi was Apollo's shrine, and Apollo was the god of truth in the Olympian pantheon. About Scolander, the narrator writes:

> I have never known anyone who could look so present and perceptive as Scolander. He manifested the extreme opposite of absent-mindedness and distraction, of preoccupation or daydreaming—traits which the average person so readily attributed to the artist. . . .
>
> Those eyes of his were presence itself. They were large, wide-open, empty, and well-ventilated shafts of apperception through which things, seen clearly and entirely unmodified, just as they were, could be poured into the mill of thought. (*Ds*, 1149)

Those who live consciously in the first reality do not approach the world with an intent to change it. They do not seek to re-form reality in order to overcome the exigencies of life; rather, they meet the "aimless variety of life" (*Ds*, 493) or the "continual delicate vacillations of reality" as they occur. Mary K., introduced early in the novel as a person living in reality, has lost one of her legs in a tram accident, is fitted with a prosthesis, and is instructed to practice walking, alone, daily. But while the struggle to learn to walk again is difficult, an *aristeia* on the order of that attributed to Homer's heroes, it does not represent her darkest time: she understands "the hardest part of all" as a

> terrible necessity that had descended upon her while she had still lain in the hospital in Vienna. That was: to spread this disaster over time; to make an event that had taken seconds an institution which would go on for years; not to stray back to the time before the accident, to those last unsuspecting hours just shortly before the debacle; not to ask herself: "How was it possible?" but to say to herself that this was the way it was now. It was necessary for her to stretch the horror out over duration, to consume it in small portions, to assimilate it, and finally to transform it into practical life—as she was doing here and now. (*Ds*, 33–34)

While Mary understood that she had to meet the tragedy forthrightly, it was the outward reality of seeing shoes in a store window that propelled her forward to the Munich clinic and thus to the *aristeia:* "Her eyes remained dry. Her misery had vanished. She suddenly grasped the grandeur of her situation, and so her hour came; so she became capable of receiving its command" (*Ds*, 34). Like Scolander, Mary K. has an impact, by example, on those living in second reality. But whereas Scolander appears only once (although he is mentioned several times, especially by Schlaggenberg), Mary is given a prominent place in the story. The chapter in which Mary is featured is placed in the exact center of the novel and is entitled "Rachel's Triumph."

In *The Demons* authentic human existence represents a conscious and comprehending awareness of the world and of life. Authentic human community—social order—can only be achieved where human beings like Mary K. forthrightly meet the endless vacillations that reality presents. It cannot rest upon what is common—race or class, for example—but instead must rest upon "what is not common, upon the singular, the personal, the noncommunicable qualities that each [person] possesses; upon what makes him irreplaceable. Otherwise the community has no lasting quality and degenerates into commonness, crudeness, baseness" (*Ds*, 494). True human community depends upon, requires even, individual apperception of the world; only upon this individual and personal apperception can authentic, dependable, stable relationships—of love, of friendship, of political community—be built. The degeneration of social order into crudeness and baseness ultimately culminates in mutual hatred and murder.

If a person exists in a healthy relationship with the world, that person is apperceiving—consciously apprehending, envisioning, or understanding—the world, reality, as it presents itself. If a person refuses to apperceive the world, then that person is actively and consciously refusing to understand or comprehend the reality by an act of *Apperzeptions-Verweigerung*. For Doderer this refusal leads to a choice to live in second reality. This refusal to apperceive is similar to, in fact, very nearly identical with, Jean-Paul Sartre's understanding of *mauvaise foi*. Sartre writes: "Bad faith apprehends evidence but it is resigned in advance to not being fulfilled by this evidence, to not being persuaded and transformed into good faith. . . . Once this mode of being has been realized, it is as difficult to get out of it as to wake oneself up; *bad faith is a type of being in the world,* like waking or dreaming, which by itself tends to perpetuate itself."[21] If individuals refuse to apperceive, their refusal has consequences for their relationship to the world and to others; ultimately they will be unable to establish authentic contact with others. The real danger—the danger to society and to the community—occurs when the individual who refuses to apperceive becomes what Albert Camus has called in *L'Homme Révolté* "the metaphysical rebel." Metaphysical rebellion is "the movement by which man protests against his condition and against the whole of creation. It is metaphysical because it contests the ends of man and of creation. The slave protests against the condition in which he finds himself within his state of slavery; the metaphysical rebel protests against the condition in which he finds himself as a man. . . . [He] . . . declares that he is frustrated by the universe."[22] In Doderer's terms, the metaphysical rebel, whom Hofrat von Gürtzner-Gontard, Geyrenhoff's former boss, calls the revolutionary, aims to stop the "continual delicate vacillations of reality," because they are contemptible. All reality for the revolutionary is a sum of trivial facts; none of them is definitive, unchangeable, or representative of "permanent laws which life always spontaneously follows"; all are subject to improvement. "'Seen from such an angle,'" Gürtzner-Gontard continues,

21. Sartre, *Being and Nothingness,* 68. Emphasis added.
22. Camus, *The Rebel,* 23.

"this life necessarily becomes only a question of arrangement, of proper rearrangement, rather, of rational classification, of will power, order (as he sees it), and efficiency. All revolutionary programs and persons necessarily have this rationalistic trait—which is one of their attractions—and suffer from the same ignorance of the stubbornness, the weight, the coercion of life's normal relationships, intellectual relationships included. Such persons have never felt the importance of these because all such normalities are parched and dead within them. Thus you might say that a priori abstraction is the mother of all revolutionaries." (*Ds*, 492–93)

After Geyrenhoff begins to understand the revolutionary nature of Schlaggenberg's obsession, he criticizes Schlaggenberg's attempt to impose order not only upon relations between the sexes but also on life in general. Schlaggenberg's second reality does not simply exist side by side with the primary reality, for in all its aspects it opposes the primary reality of life. "Order is in itself praiseworthy and valuable," Geyrenhoff tells Schlaggenberg,

"we agree on that! But I've noticed that you, for a long time now, forever and a day in fact, have been chiefly occupied with making order. In everything. A few minutes ago you were talking about order again, saying that the thing [Schlaggenberg's project] had not 'created any essential order' for you, or however you put it. There are pedants who turn into a strange type of domestic tyrant . . . in regard to their own biographies, so to speak. They insist that their life-stories fit into a predetermined orderly pattern, and eliminate anything for which there is no room in that pattern. They hope to construct a Tower of Babel to the God of Order out of the building-materials of life. . . . Of course they don't want anything new, any additions; the slightest disturbance and things will be dangling 'like a broken wing.' The smallest nothing upsets the 'growing oneness and tranquility' of such a life. This oneness is nothing but the rigid pattern, the establishment of a second life, and anti-life." (*Ds*, 375)

In the attempt to impose order upon life and reality, second reality, or the anti-life, is rationalistically constructed. It is clear, however, that for those who set out to reconstruct reality along ideological lines, the first reality does not disappear. While the metaphysical rebel rejects the standards of humanity and human dignity, he has not resigned from the human race. He experiences a bifurcated existence; on the one hand, his body and mind remain rooted in the first reality that he has refused to apperceive, and on the other hand, he must wear blinkers that permit him to deny the "real constitution of the world" (D, 857). The medieval manuscript of Ruodlieb von der Vläntsch had expressed his simultaneous experience of the first and second realities when he dreamed that he was made half of wood. "There," says Stangeler, the translator of the medieval manuscript,

> "you have the collision of two realities. He could still remember the first, but already the second reality possessed him. . . . That is the modern experience, the clash between a first and a second reality, between which no bridge exists, and no common language, although all the individual words that make up the two languages are common to each. Lord Achaz expresses it in the following words: 'A dreme, when that overcometh thee and thou art alone wyth it, wyth thy dreme and vision, alle els escapeth thee and thou art loste.'" (*Ds*, 1019)

The capacity to recognize and even experience the primary reality of life while existing in second reality is confirmed by Schlaggenberg, Doderer's paradigm of the truly modern, twentieth-century ideologue who would impose his system of order on reality. While pursuing his *Dicke-Damen-Doctrinar-Sexualität* project, he met Mary K. He describes this experience to the narrator:

> "When I first caught sight of Mary K. I was conscious of a bad clouding of my sight. I recognized her excellence, recognized the sort of person I had before me—and yet I could not really see her. Do you understand that? Apperception remained shallow, like shallow hasty breathing. The object perceived did not penetrate, did not penetrate into me. I felt as if I were callused, covered with a horny skin. Every real apperception is not only a contact and superficial mingling of inner and outer; it is an interpenetration of both. . . . But in those crucial moments I lacked the capacity to be penetrated. I was capable only of a kind of bordering, fringe contact; only in that limited way was apperception possible for me. And I had to recognize that I had lost my sexual impartiality and was living in a second reality" (Oh, Stangeler!) "as everyone who pursues a 'type' becomes the idiotic scarecrow of his own displaced sexuality: a constant anticipation that is never attained. . . . [S]ex is the greatest window of our apperception, and if this window clouds, all others will soon suffer from cataracts. Half blind, you will peer out at all things only through the narrow slit of some program or other, always anticipating what ought to be. And in the end you'll call it an ideal." (*Ds*, 1076–77)

In times of panic and social upheaval, individuals who can no longer endure the variety that life presents them choose to rebel against all of reality. "The revolutionary flees from what is hardest for him to bear, the aimless variety of life; he seeks perfection, which in the world of his trivialities can at best mean completeness" (*Ds*, 493). Smashing all previous human standards, such rebels are no longer limited by the standards of the human community. At this point, Gürtzner-Gontard points out that

> it is others who have to endure him. The abandoned, highly concrete task of his own life, with which he has been unable to cope in a personal and individual fashion, has of course to be consigned to oblivion, and along with it the capacity for remembering in general, memory as the foundation of the personality. When that happens, the slogan is born; and that same hour marks the burial of immediacy, of concreteness, of quick measures, of direct relationship to inimical or friendly persons. (*Ds*, 491)

Gürtzner-Gontard here reveals that individuality, and its openness to confronting the concrete tasks of life, i.e., the capacity to confront the vicissitudes of life and overcome them, provides the real basis for direct relationships "to inimical or friendly persons." One is here reminded of Mary K. and her *aristeia* as the model of a person who lives in full openness to reality, who refuses to be defeated by tragic accidents, and who can therefore establish authentic relationships to others. In reordering life to an ideal, the revolutionary chooses to forget his past. The political direction of these so-called "philosophies" of the twentieth century matters little, because as Gürtzner-Gontard argues,

> "in a 'racially pure' society every blockhead and brute who has been unable to get anywhere will at least be able to achieve the rank of 'Aryan.' Take an 'idealist' headed in another direction: the proletarian. He too can distinguish himself by his very lowliness. In the one case you have an assumed community of race, in the other of class—it's the same difference. Classes can become races, and vice versa. . . . In both cases the self-assurance necessary to support weakness is drawn from a common fund, whether race-consciousness or class-consciousness. Both produce the same amount of animal warmth." (*Ds*, 494)

In the end, ideologues of both right and left attempt to kill each other, requiring that millions of human beings suffer and die for the sake of their own rebellious inauthenticity.

GEORG VON GEYRENHOFF'S SECOND REALITY:
THE HOBBYHORSE CHRONICLE OF *DIE UNSRIGEN*

---

When a man gives himself up to the government of a ruling passion, —or, in
other words, when his HOBBY-HORSE grows headstrong, —farewell cool
reason and fair discretion!

~ LAURENCE STERNE, *TRISTRAM SHANDY, GENTLEMAN*

To illustrate in some detail the components of second reality as they
manifest themselves in a particular character, we focus on the nature
and development of the character Georg von Geyrenhoff—the ultimately "revised" first-person narrator. Unlike Schlaggenberg, who constructs his *Dicke-Damen-Doctrinar-Sexualität,* or his fascist nephew
Doktor Kurt Körger—both members of *die Unsrigen*—Geyrenhoff is
not living in a recognizably ideological second reality. Geyrenhoff's
second reality is blander, more banal, and characterized primarily as
obtuseness: a clouding of perception. But when members of a society
are imperceptive and obtuse, the purveyors of the organized ideologies
are provided a fertile ground for proffering "animal warmth." Thus
despite its seeming banality, Geyrenhoff's second reality grows from
his *Apperzeptions-Verweigerung* and issues in social and political
consequences.

One is led to believe by the "Overture" to *The Demons* that the novel
will essentially be a chronicle of *die Unsrigen.* As one proceeds through
the book, however, it becomes apparent that the narrator is not to be
trusted. Geyrenhoff says of himself in the "Overture":

> I remained partially or completely ignorant of many matters as events
> proceeded, sometimes of crucial matters. So that now—after it is all
> over and I am sitting here in Schlaggenberg's "last studio" preparing to
> summarize and revise the whole story—I would feel fraudulent were I
> to attempt to represent myself as less stupid and ignorant than I actu-
> ally was, at least in those segments which I relate as an eyewitness and
> in which, therefore, I myself appear. . . . Although I myself was never
> actually involved in the events (that would have been the last straw), I
> was still obliged to depict myself in a corner here or there. . . .
>
> Today, of course, "knowing the whole story," I have all the proverbial
> benefits of hindsight. (*Ds,* 7)

The retelling of Geyrenhoff's story, however, will reveal that even with the "proverbial benefits of hindsight" he is still deluded. As I have noted above, an omniscient narrator, in the "end," revises the Geyrenhoff of the Overture.

Geyrenhoff tells us early in the novel that he has just moved out to the Nineteenth District of Vienna, Döbling, and that he has fallen in with a group of individuals that he calls *die Unsrigen.* He informs us that he is a pensioner, having retired from the civil service when he received part of his inheritance that had just been released in England after "sequestration" during World War I. Geyrenhoff is a bachelor with no cares and plenty of time; and in order to give himself something to do, he decides to chronicle the activities of *die Unsrigen* (*Ds,* 5–6).

The main plot begins on November 20, 1926, when Geyrenhoff, traveling in a taxi to a meeting with a former civil service colleague, sees Kajetan von Schlaggenberg on a traffic island. and the taxi driver very nearly runs Schlaggenberg down. This incident marks for Geyrenhoff the beginning of a new segment of his life. He says: "Actually, the new segment of my life, my secession, I might put it, was already beginning" (*Ds,* 48). The "secession" from the cares of life, from having a job with responsibilities, represents the first manifestation of his second reality. The illusion of secession enables him to conceive his chronicle project, throughout which he expects to take the role of an impartial observer, in keeping a diary "for a whole group of persons" (*Ds,* 6). That he "intends" to observe the activities of a group of socially diverse individuals as though he were not involved, as though he himself were not a participant in the group, hints that he is living in a second reality. Even though Geyrenhoff knows many of the members of *die Unsrigen,* and even assumes that some of them are his friends, his intention reveals a difficulty with relationships. In fact, he only trusts his former superior in the civil service, Hofrat von Gürtzner-Gontard. Even though these early indications of second reality—secession and nonparticipation—are present in the novel, it is only when Geyrenhoff calls attention to apperceptual problems affecting his chronicle that the reader is asked to recognize them as well. For example, remembering from a much later point in time his preparations for breakfast with Gürtzner-Gontard on the morning of July 15, 1927, Geyrenhoff thinks: "During those days I was in a state of considerable distraction. When I examined myself, I became aware of a distinct slackening of energies. . . . It actually seemed to me that my conception of my surroundings was becoming blurred, as though I were becoming the exact opposite of a man like Scolander" (*Ds,* 1216).

One manifestation of Geyrenhoff's second reality is his inability to see accurately (and hence authentically to chronicle) what is taking place around him. This is particularly true of his misjudgment of Stangeler. Gürtzner-Gontard, to whom Geyrenhoff has gone in order to hear an assessment of the general situation from a person who is outside *die Unsrigen* and thus a trustworthy authority for him, lectures his former subordinate on the nature of the revolutionary ideology and second realities, a lecture that he admits to having plagiarized from Stangeler, a member of *die Unsrigen*. When Gürtzner-Gontard confesses this plagiarism, Geyrenhoff realizes that he has seriously misjudged Stangeler and thus that his own judgment is impaired. Geyrenhoff writes:

> I cherished a virtual formula which amounted to: "Stangeler is to blame for everything." And in fact he was constantly upsetting me—by his incomprehensibility in general; by what I called the crack in his nature, and should have quickly seen as a profound gulf; by what seemed to be his imperiousness, so that no matter how you tried to jolt him he would always go on talking a blue streak, producing the same worthless drivel; by his unsteadiness, his being all twisted into knots, denuded of his real abilities. . . .
>
> But today I know far more about it all. I know that . . . it was he (I once said angrily of him that he lived "as if torn to shreds") who kept me, after I had come into my inheritance and resigned from the civil service, from growing into a careful, dignified old gentleman. (*Ds*, 49)

Clearly, Geyrenhoff could understand neither the language nor the life of the young historian.

The most serious problem of failed apperception, however, occurs with Geyrenhoff's inability to communicate directly, or establish an unmediated relationship, with Friederike von Ruthmayr. Whenever he encounters Friederike, he perceives her only as a "noble, ornamental fish" that floats up to him from behind a pane of glass. He observes that "I gradually learned after all to understand the language of fish and to lip-read the meaning of a mouth that remained essentially mute behind the painful partition that separated us, the wall of crystal. She floats up to it, the eyes directed upon me; she speaks, and yet she remains mute. *She is incapable of composed, coherent speech*" (*Ds*, 1162; emphasis added). Having alienated himself from himself, Geyrenhoff attributes to Friederike the inability to communicate, failing to understand that the real problem lay in his own refusal of apperception.

The reader is not given very much information about Geyrenhoff's life prior to 1926, when he moves to Döbling. We do know, however, only after Geyrenhoff himself remembers, that as a teenager—aged sixteen—he met the Countess Claire von Neudegg and that this encounter had fateful consequences for his ability to establish authentic relationships with women. In fact, this meeting blocked his apperception in such a way that he was later unable to experience Friederike Ruthmayr as a human being.[23] In a moment of remembrance he writes:

> I had met the baroness for the first time in my mother's home, had been ordered to accompany her downstairs and open the garden gate for her. . . . At the carriage she turned and extended her hand. As she did so, she assumed an expression of *utterly inimitable arrogance and inordinately stupid impertinence.* Yet there was not the slightest pretext or reason for her to act this way toward a humble high-school boy—whom was she trying to impress? The senseless outrageousness of this conduct shocked me so thoroughly that for days afterwards I had a kind of aftertaste of it, as though there were some spoiled food lying in my stomach. Exactly this sort of lingering feeling remained after my talk with Levielle on the Graben. . . . [A]fterwards I became fully aware of his *quite mysterious arrogance,* although I had sensed something of it right at the beginning of the conversation. How did these people get that way? I asked myself; and as a schoolboy I had actually asked myself precisely the same question during those days after the incident with Baroness Neudegg. To this day I have never found any answer to this question. (*Ds,* 113–14; emphasis added)

Even as he is being projected into second reality by Baroness Neudegg, the young Geyrenhoff is conscious of the ludicrousness of her behavior and questions her arrogance. The recollection that he had asked the question of the baroness in the past and of Levielle in the present, and that he found no answer to the question then or now, represents the beginning of his recovery of apperception.

> Later, after the war, I met Claire Neudegg, now Countess Charagiel, somewhere again. . . . I gave her the appropriate greetings. She thanked me in exactly the manner in which she had once thanked the high-school boy. Time seemed to have left no mark upon her in any sense. She was a beautiful woman. But I was no longer a lowly, adoring high-school boy.

23. As we will see below, the barb that was implanted in Geyrenhoff by the baroness dissolves as he falls genuinely in love with Frederike Ruthmayr.

Nevertheless, she thrust me back to my sixteenth year; she could do that. And so it seemed as though time had left no mark upon me either. (*Ds*, 114–15)

The arrogance with which Baroness Neudegg treated a starstruck schoolboy began a long period of blocked apperception for Geyrenhoff. It is clear that the episode with Claire von Neudegg, even though he had first met her in 1900, exercised an enduring psychic influence on him in early 1927. Since that first encounter, his development was arrested, or one might say that his openness to the "continual delicate vacillations of reality" had been closed. "Time had left no mark" upon him either. Only when Geyrenhoff is confronted with the same type of experience—with Levielle on the Graben—twenty-seven years later does he recall the first. Despite the expectation, in a second reality, of being able to alter one's surroundings and even human nature, one cannot change even oneself.

On the day Geyrenhoff began writing his chronicle (November 21, 1926) he records a "strange" and "sibylline" occurrence. He writes:

> I was sifting through these notes when I suddenly sensed some unpleasant ray touching my spirit, if not my actual body, although but a moment before I had been in a state of perfect well-being. And while still inwardly crying out to myself: "Nonsense—what can be the matter?" (this is how we always suppress what we do not want to face; we force it down, compress it and thereby intensify it), I found I could no longer stay in my chair. I bounded up from the desk, walked to the middle of the room, and as though quite by chance raised my eyes . . . into the upper emptiness of space where we are surely not in the habit of looking. I peered at the spot where ceiling and wall met, for the sensation came from up there. That was the seat of it. The wall was quite bare, but it was just as if the portrait of a woman hung there, a most beautiful woman with dark braids, whose face looked down into my room, into my life and doings, into my notes, my associates, the whole animated hollowness of my existence at that time, with scorn, with contempt, and a boundless, stupid arrogance, so that everything . . . turned as pallid as bleached bone and literally perished in utter ludicrousness. Everything, not to speak of my first feeble efforts at keeping a chronicle.
>
> It was gone in a trice. No name had come to my mind, no person, but only someone's essence, as it were. . . . The link to consciousness was not forged at this time. It was not until after my . . . walk with Herr Levielle down the Graben on March 25, 1927—Annunciation Day—

that something made me think of the Baroness Claire Neudegg, later Countess Charagiel; not until then did I realize that she had already been present in my mind that November day, and thus that my thoughts had traveled far back into my youth, to my sixteenth year. (*Ds*, 51–52)

This is one of those dreams "which are really no longer dreams but rather insights" that play such an important role in Geyrenhoff's emergence from second reality. The dream insinuates into Geyrenhoff's subconscious the image of Baroness Neudegg, which calls into question "the whole animated hollowness of [his] existence." It is important that this is a partially recollected psychic disturbance; that Geyrenhoff emphasizes that "the link to consciousness was not forged at this time," and would not be until four months later, because he was still living in second reality. In retrospect or in remembering, however, Geyrenhoff makes the link with consciousness; or is it the omniscient narrator—a revised Geyrenhoff who has emerged from second reality, plunged back into the messiness and flux of life's affairs, and is now open to the past that had been suppressed by the chronicler Geyrenhoff—who forges the link with consciousness?

Elizabeth Hesson argues that "only a forced confrontation with empirical reality . . . will allow [an individual living in a second reality] to break free of it."[24] Borrowing from Gütersloh the saying "die Tiefe ist aussen" (the depth is outside), Doderer has Stangeler murmur it to himself as one of Scolander's statements.[25] It is the depth of external reality—the depth from which the community of Being emerges—in which consciousness participates that will intrude upon the consciousness of one living in second reality and will ultimately make it possible for the person to escape or emerge from it. In Geyrenhoff's case, the emergence from second reality into the open consciousness of life—the first reality—may be attributed to several factors: (1) disturbances on the order of daydreams or "visitations" that well up from the depths of Geyrenhoff's psyche that exists in the *metaxy* (despite his second reality hobbyhorse) in continuity with the Anaximandrian Apeiron; (2) chance occurrences—"vacillations of reality"—that intensify the disturbances in consciousness and lead Geyrenhoff to crucial information about members of *die Unsrigen*, especially about Quapp Schlaggenberg; (3) the fall from the hobbyhorse of his chronicling and subsequent

24. Hesson, *Twentieth Century Odyssey*, 13.
25. Ibid., 66, and Doderer, *The Demons*, 1186.

involvement with the financial affairs of Quapp and Friederike Ruthmayr; and (4) falling in love with Friederike Ruthmayr.[26]

May 15, 1927, was a crucial day in the life of Georg von Geyrenhoff. On the evening of Saturday, May 14, the Siebenscheins held a table-tennis tea for *die Unsrigen*. Geyrenhoff arrived late to the event and left early to attend the opera *Der Rosenkavalier* with Friederike Ruthmayr. At the tea, Geyrenhoff became obsessed with the meaning of Körger's neck, which had become for him a symbol of the fascist ideas on which Körger was holding forth. By this point in the story, Geyrenhoff had begun to feel that he was losing control not only of his attempt through his chronicling to impose an artificially rational order upon *die Unsrigen,* but also of the events of his life. Ironically, Geyerenhoff's recognition of the loss of control while in second reality leads to a recognition that control of reality is not even possible. Since Geyrenhoff had already been feeling "out of control"—suddenly recognizing "my imperative need to talk, to talk myself out, and to be contradicted by someone who mattered, who could apply an impartial standard to my confusion"—he had made an appointment for Sunday morning, May 15, with Hofrat Gürtzner-Gontard (*Ds,* 484). "I awoke the next morning," May 15, Geyrenhoff begins the chapter "On the Open Road," "feeling as if I had been inwardly uncoupled, like a passenger who by some fantastic mischance has been forgotten in the compartment of a sleeping car; he awakens to find himself far out of town, alone in a wilderness of sidings, instead of at the railroad station" (*Ds,* 477). The condition of being uncoupled represents a paradox. On the one hand, if one is living in the first reality, such a condition may lead to the desire to make order, to impose order on reality through the construction of a second reality. The estrangement between Schlaggenberg and his wife, Camy, for example, led to his attempt to impose order on his sex life by building his system of *Dicke-Damen-Doctrinar-Sexualität.* On the other hand, if one has already constructed and is living in a second reality, the condition signals not only a bubbling up from the depth of the consciousness that still exists in the *metaxy* but also a disturbance in the anticipated comfort that one expects from the supposed order of a second reality. In Geyrenhoff's

26. Of course, a person who lives in second reality has never left the first reality and cannot, therefore, "escape" from second into first reality. The change occurs within his consciousness of reality and his subsequent acceptance of the conditions of human life in the *metaxy.* What changes is his rejection of *Apperzeptions-Verweigerung,* or his blocked apperception.

case, the uncoupled condition represents one of the factors he later identifies as leading to the fall from his hobbyhorse.

Lying in bed awake and thinking about the events of the previous evening, Geyrenhoff is haunted by the image of Körger's neck.

> It danced away from me. . . . Now the neck floated jellylike toward me again. I could not simply chase it away, blow it away, wave it away with a gesture. I had somehow something to do with it. It had already become a kind of authority which I myself had virtually recognized during my walk through the fog—overwhelmed and wearied as I had been by the whole stage-setting. That was the neck's power. I became conscious this morning, with gloomy uneasiness, of the dangers and personal afflictions of a new life—which I had entered not yesterday but months before.
>
> And now I wanted to walk out on it again, although in the next moment I recognized that the impulse was a desire to make order, like my friend Schlaggenberg; that I was on the point of making such order and badly needed it. (*Ds*, 478–79)

It is apparent that Geyrenhoff here is tempted by the fascism of his nephew Körger and the order it proffers, i.e., the rational ordering of life according to an abstract principle, and to "walk out on it [first reality] again." In principle the order represented by Körger's neck and Kajetan von Schlaggenberg's system are the same: both are rooted in the refusal to apperceive the nature of reality itself with its attendant uncertainties. Clearly, Geyrenhoff is in a state of confusion and transition. Does he want order in his chronicle like the order that Schlaggenberg is attempting to establish in his *Chronique Scandaleuse, Dicke-Damen-Doctrinar-Sexualität*? Or does he want the genuine order that is open to "continual vacillations"? Hence, Geyrenhoff's appointment with Gürtzner-Gontard to be "contradicted by someone who mattered."

Pondering the events and the connections that had been revealed at the previous evening's gathering of *die Unsrigen*, Geyrenhoff could not understand what was going on, even though he had all the facts at hand. What Geyrenhoff could not understand was the plot by Levielle to steal Quapp's inheritance and who was involved, but subsequent events of this day—May 15—would bring an end to his hobbyhorse chronicle. As the chronicling ends, Geyrenhoff begins to emerge from second reality. After the early-morning disturbance, Geyrenhoff visits Gürtzner-Gontard to talk himself out. Gürtzner-Gontard accuses his former subordinate of being a revolutionary and lectures him about revolutionaries, revolutionary ideologies, and their connections to second reality. Moreover, he reveals to Geyrenhoff that he has learned all of this from René von Stangeler; this revelation further disturbs Geyrenhoff, because he realizes that he has completely misunderstood and misjudged Stangeler. The feeling with which he awoke that morning, "that he had been inwardly uncoupled," seems to presage a reemergence into reality, with its vacillations and uncertainties that had led to his second reality in the first place. This feeling was reinforced by the visit to Gürtzner-Gontard.

After leaving Gürtzner-Gontard's, Geyrenhoff is strolling on the Graben when he chances to meet Alois Gach whom he knows from the war. While they are talking Quapp Schlaggenberg comes along, and Gach notes a remarkable resemblance between Quapp and Captain Ruthmayr, Gach's former commanding officer. Geyrenhoff is surprised by this, because he too, while drifting off to sleep one evening, had pondered the same resemblance. Gach tells him that he had been present at the captain's death and that on his deathbed Ruthmayr had made out a will leaving a special set of funds to a daughter he had fathered out of wedlock. Ruthmayr's daughter turns out to be Quapp Schlaggenberg, and her mother was none other than the Baroness Claire von Neudegg. Gach had taken the will to Financial Counselor Levielle, who put it in a secret drawer of his bureau. Nothing was heard of the will again until Geyrenhoff finds out about it from Gach. It is at this point, after his chance encounter with Gach and while walking in the Third District, that Geyrenhoff realizes he has fallen from the hobbyhorse of his chronicling. He says that "I refused to let my imagination play over what Gach had unexpectedly revealed to me at the restaurant table. I was no longer a chronicler. My role as such had come to an end today. I had fallen from my hobbyhorse. The fall was followed by a sense of emptiness" (*Ds*, 844).

The fourth event of May 15 occurs after his chance meeting with Gach and while he is strolling along Reissner Strasse. Geyrenhoff is accosted by Mucki Langingen and Prince Alfons Croix. The prince invites Geyrenhoff to his house for a drink and during the conversation introduces the topic of Countess Claire Charagiel (née Baroness Claire von Neudegg). Alfons Croix reveals that the countess had died the past winter and that her father, Baron von Neudegg, had just died this spring—1927.[27]

---

27. These deaths will lead to other developments that we cannot include in the story of Geyrenhoff's fall. Because the Baron dies, Jan Herzka inherits his castle and a medieval manuscript; Herzka hires Stangeler to translate the manuscript from which Stangeler develops his idea of the "second reality." Stangeler then communicates his theories about revolutionary ideologies and second realities to Hofrat von Gürtzner-Gontard, who in turn enlightens Geyrenhoff on Sunday, May 15.

The events of May 15—a disturbing dream/daydream upon awakening, a conversation with Hofrat Gürtzner-Gontard, a chance meeting with Alois Gach, and another chance encounter with Prince Alfons Croix—all lead Geyrenhoff to understand that his chronicling has ended. Upon leaving Gach on that Sunday afternoon, he reflects: "Now, for the first time since the morning, I felt a sense of everything that had happened, was about to or could happen, stacked up beneath me. And I suddenly became aware that I would never fully understand the group whose activities I was attempting to chronicle" (*Ds*, 845). On May 16 Geyrenhoff awakens with the feeling that a gulf had opened between yesterday's awakening and today's. "But the real gulf," he thinks,

> was formed by my evening with Alfons Croix and Mucki. That was the deepest part, a gently glowing hollow in which the previous excitement of the day had come to rest. But this hollow, shut within the great gray stony masses of surrounding existence, to which I had suddenly and accidentally penetrated, gave me assurance of unknown values in this world around me, of potential new fragrances—gave me for the moment real life, true hope.
>
> With this new *élan*, I sprang out of bed. The *élan* remained with me for part of the day. I looked at my chronicle, my hobbyhorse, and knew that I would never again mount into its ridiculous little saddle. (*Ds*, 958–9)

He continues:

> At any rate, this preoccupation with affairs that were being thrown my way, that were not my own and were already becoming my own, engendered in me a curious sense of well-being. As a chronicler I was finished. But I was rather pleased to regard myself as an actor; it seemed to me that I already stood on a higher plane of life. . . . As a chronicler I had labored in vain to get at the center of things. . . . Now, however, I had an inkling of higher forms of action; in fact, of what action really was. That was what writing had brought me to. *Primum scribere deinde vivere*. Write first, then live. The inverse and original form of this proverb was only a maxim for reporters, for at best crude naturalists. It did not do justice to the true mechanism of the mind.
>
> Now, however, I was enjoying my insight into that mechanism. My concern for the affairs of another, which were becoming my own affairs, did me good; while my own original concerns were beginning to look alien to me. Alienate yourself from yourself, and soon nothing will be alien to you any longer! Whereas previously I had raised opinions and attitudes like seedlings in flower beds . . . ; whereas previously I had

cultivated tastes and even sympathies and antipathies—I now realized that all the onetime roots were established very shallowly in ground which would just as readily and indifferently have nourished things entirely different. For my part, I gladly renounced my specialties and my whole "chronicle," abandoned my pet theories, sympathies, antipathies, et al. Concern for the affairs of others—was it not a form of appropriation, conquest, taking possession? True, and yet this same *cura aliena* now seemed to be of higher worth.

It animated me, it made me happy. (*Ds*, 963–64)

Geyrenhoff's chronicling had arisen from his urge to stand over against the actions that are occurring around him as an "objective observer" and to make order, to impose order upon the life activities of *die Unsrigen*. When Geyrenhoff is led by his chronicling to become involved in the affairs of others, to act on behalf of others, he can no longer maintain his "objectivity," his "indifference" to life; he must act not only on behalf of his friend Quapp but also out of his sense of fairness. At this point he begins to emerge from the second reality of his chronicling, but his full reentrance into life occurs only when he uncovers the whole story of Quapp's inheritance, secures that inheritance for her, tells Friederike Ruthmayr of Quapp, introduces Quapp to Friederike, and throughout the foregoing falls genuinely in love with Friederike.[28]

Perhaps a few remarks on Geyrenhoff's relation to Friederike Ruthmayr are in order here. As we have seen already, Geyrenhoff is prevented from apperceiving Frau Ruthmayr by the second reality into which the Baroness von Neudegg had projected him. This blocked apperception causes Geyrenhoff to perceive Friederike as a fish behind a crystal wall, but after he has fallen from his hobbyhorse and involved himself in the affairs of Quapp, he realizes that he must discuss Quapp with Friederike, for Quapp is, after all, the daughter of Friederike's late husband. Geyrenhoff knew that he was developing a relationship with Friederike, but he mistakenly believes that Friederike will be his salvation from Claire Neudegg. Still seeking salvation from the baroness, he writes:

Friederike alone, she alone could heal me, could draw out the wasp's sting that had been imbedded deep in my youthful soul, that time. She, Friederike, would have the maternal hand to grope for and find it, the

28. In consideration of length, I have not discussed many other details and characters in the story of Geyrenhoff uncovering the facts of Quapp's inheritance and then securing it for her.

sting which was unnoticeable to others but which still upon occasion smarted bitterly in me. Now I knew why I had so long remained a bachelor. And a crystal wall, a glass pane, was receding from me and dissolving into thin air, and from behind I felt the breath of warmth I had never experienced, warmth that for seconds rose to a burning and then was swiftly repressed again. (*Ds*, 1090–91)

In telling Friederike about Quapp and arranging Friederike's financial affairs with Bank Director Altschul (Financial Counselor Levielle has fled for parts unknown after the revelation that he suppressed Captain Ruthmayr's last will), Geyrenhoff comes to several realizations. First, while listening to Friederike speak of her life with Captain Ruthmayr and her life since his death (during which time she deferred to Financial Counselor Levielle because of her own insecurities), he realizes for the first time that he is truly hearing what Friederike is telling him. "Suddenly the thought seized me furiously—furiously, because a moment before my rage had been directed against Levielle— that there was no crystal wall, that nothing separated me from Friederike except the Charagiel woman—that she had been the wall all along, nothing else" (*Ds*, 1166). Second, he realizes that he and Friederike have fallen in love and now share a future together; this is also noticed by Bank Director Altschul. "As Altschul bade us good-by, something happened that was perfectly plain and yet can scarcely be put into words. He united us with a look; he performed a syn-opsis, and with palpable benevolence. It left me with a feeling of confusion. . . . Not only Friederike was returning to life; I too was doing so. We both entered it at the same moment" (*Ds*, 1167).

Finally, Geyrenhoff experiences an emergence from the sphere of Claire Charagiel's influence. As he explained Quapp's legacy to Friederike, he was healed.

So I told her about Quapp. I explained the legacy entirely in Levielle's terms—"rediscovered" testament and all. I said that Quapp's mother was the Baroness Charagiel, and made it clear that the affair had taken place before Ruthmayr and she, Friederike, had ever met. And while I was thus letting the cat out of the bag, something altogether enormous and unexpected happened: it carried with it the sting that Claire Neudegg had left in my flesh. Even as I spoke I became insensitive, quite neutral, toward the whole matter. I could scarcely grasp it. My body, sitting in the chair, was healed down to its ultimate depths, down to the central core of life somewhere deep within. (*Ds*, 1167)

In summary, we have learned several things about Geyrenhoff. First, he was an unreliable narrator, who planned to revise his chronicle but instead was revised by himself in the person of the omniscient narrator finishing the "chronicle" in 1955. Indeed, after Geyrenhoff emerges from his second reality, he has become a reliable narrator and could thus revise not only his manuscript but also himself. Second, not until 1927 does he consciously trace his apperceptual obtuseness to his experience with Baroness Neudegg. Apparently he had not even realized that such a problem existed until then (although he had sensed it in his dreams). Third, Geyrenhoff's experience of second reality—between his remembrance of the baroness's arrogance and his emergence from second reality on July 15, 1927, the day that the Palace of Justice was burned by ideologues of the left—includes several dimensions. Until his fall from the hobbyhorse, he was unable to understand others (Stangeler, for instance); he could not make authentic emotional contact with Friederike, and he perceived her to be speaking the language of a fish; after November 1926, he experienced more and more frequently moments of psychic dislocation and uneasiness, the depth of his consciousness bubbling up in "dreams" and "visitations" that he later understood as insights; he continued to sense the real events occurring around him without understanding their meaning; and, finally, he could only understand what had happened to him when he was in second reality after he had become conscious again of life and of the love of life as meaningful.

Geyrenhoff's reentry into life was accomplished through (a) being thrust into participating in the financial affairs of Quapp and Friederike—affairs that were characterized by the fact that they meant something, unlike his chronicling (taken up because he believed he had, and wanted, no cares); (b) chronicling itself, which led to confusion that needed explanation from the outside; and (c) being contradicted from the outside—"die Tiefe ist aussen"—by Gürtzner-Gontard, which led him to recognize his own biographical inveracity. Combined, his practical financial activity on Friederike's behalf, his activity of securing Quapp's inheritance for her, and his being contradicted from outside led Geyrenhoff to a state in which he healed himself, or in which he could at last, at the age of forty-three, face and accept the "continual delicate vacillations of reality."

REFLECTIONS

Although I have only examined a fragment of Doderer's monumental novel, we are in a position to identify several general principles about second reality—its genesis in the psyches of individuals, its characteristics in the lives of those individuals, and the possible conditions or events that may lead to an individual's extrication from its influence and reemergence into life and actual reality.

The genesis of second reality in an individual may be located in time. Even though Geyrenhoff identifies the moment that he was projected—into *Apperzeptions-Verweigerung* as a passive refusal of apperception—by Baroness Neudegg, twenty-seven years after the event we remain unsure why it happened. Did this encounter just happen to Geyrenhoff? Did the barb delivered by the inimitably arrogant baroness anesthetize the young Geyrenhoff to the "continual delicate vacillations of reality" at a particularly vulnerable age? Was young Geyrenhoff an active participant in his projection into second reality? Or was he simply overcome by the poison barb of Claire's arrogance and stupidity?

Geyrenhoff's age at the time of his encounter with the baroness seems to indicate that a crucial disturbance in the relationship between the sexes can lead into second reality, or perhaps that this disturbance supplies a more-or-less unconscious motive for one's refusing to apperceive reality if the experience occurs in adolescence or early adulthood. Geyrenhoff does write: "Now I knew why I had so long remained a bachelor." The following sentence—"And a crystal wall, a glass pane, was receding from me and dissolving into thin air, and from behind I felt the breath of warmth I had never experienced" —implies that once this knowledge became conscious, once Geyrenhoff consciously remembers the barb implanted in his youthful soul, he heals himself, not by understanding the language of a human configured as a fish, but by actually and purposefully communicating with her, using a common language.

Doderer's title, *The Demons* (*Die Dämonen*), would at least suggest that second reality can take many forms although it is essentially one mode of being rooted in *Apperzeptions-Verweigerung*. That Doderer entitled the novel after the German translation title—*Die Dämonen*—of Dostoyevsky's novel, in which the reader is directed to the demons of obsessive language and being, suggests that he meant to focus the reader's attention on that novel. What are the consequences of such a focus? If those in second reality are harassed or possessed by demons, does this possession involve a kind of submission or acquiescence on the part of the possessed? Why did it take twenty-seven years for Geyrenhoff to emerge from the cocoon of second reality? The ultimate reason for the genesis of his second reality may simply remain, as Voegelin notes about Hegel, a "secret between God and man."

*Apperzeptions-Verweigerung*—the refusal of apperception, or the refusal to apperceive—lies at the heart of the condition of living in second reality; perception is still occurring, but conscious perception—apperception—is blocked. The person living in second reality experiences deficiencies in his apperceptive apparatus; his vision is clouded and he is blinded (Schlaggenberg); he experiences a bifurcation of his psyche between something living and something dead; he is half made of wood (Lord Achaz von Neudegker and his squire, Ruodlieb von der Vläntsch); and he is blinded to the meaning of certain events and characters (Geyrenhoff). Moreover, especially with Geyrenhoff's case, came an indifference to the world; this indifference had, oddly, provided the basis for his belief that he could chronicle the affairs of *die Unsrigen* as an objective observer. As Geyrenhoff is wandering the streets after his chance meeting with Alois Gach on the afternoon of May 15, he reflects on what has already happened that day. He feels that everything that has happened or that could happen has built up beneath him and realizes that he could never completely understand the members of *die Unsrigen*, whose activities he was recording. He describes his mood:

> Indifference gripped me, but this grip was not gentle, not reassuring; it was icy, hinted at fearful terrors. I realized at once that indifference does not permit an objective view of things, as might at first appear. It blocks one's view. Indifference blinds. Nor does it remain indifference; it degenerates rapidly into disgust with life. (*Ds*, 845)

As Geyrenhoff emerges from second reality, his indifference to the world and life disappears, and his capacity for experiencing life is revitalized, as exemplified in his new relationship with Frederike Ruthmayr.

The recognition that *Apperzeptions-Verweigerung* (and its effect upon the individual's relation to the external world—he is impenetrable—and to his own biographical veracity) lies at the heart of one's pathological condition occurs only after one has extricated oneself from second reality. A person in second reality is living in a private world of his own making, what Voegelin calls the contraction of the self,[29] and

---

29. In "The Eclipse of Reality," Voegelin writes: "By an act of imagination man can

does not, therefore, participate in the community of Being held in common with fellow human beings. The extrication from second reality only occurs as a result of a dramatic confrontation of the person living in second reality with the external world. Chance events, intuited visitations, dreams, and practical affairs are all vehicles through which the external world penetrates the barricaded or contracted self. Yet these vehicles are stimuli that only make extrication possible, not inevitable. Again, we run up against the mystery: a "secret between God and man."

Living in openness to reality offers the prospect of love and community. Analyzing Albert Camus' efforts to overcome the second reality at the core of modernity, Voegelin emphasizes that in *L'Homme révolté*, Camus recognizes that the "men who despair of personal freedom . . . 'no longer believe in what exists in the world and in living man; the secret of Europe is that it no longer loves life.'"[30] Voegelin continues:

> The vision of [Camus'] cure: Revolt has reached its "midi de la pensée" [meridian of thought]—men deny themselves the right to become gods and thus relinquish the unlimited power to inflict death. . . .
>
> A note in Camus's *Carnets*, dating from about the same period, makes it clear that his self-analysis had already gone beyond the formulation of *L'Homme révolté*: "Non pas la morale mais l'accomplissement. Et il n'y a pas d'autre accomplissement que celui de l'amour, c'est-à-dire du renoncement à soi-même et de la mort au monde. Aller jusqu'au bout. *Disparaître.* Se dissoudre dans l'amour. Ce sera la force de l'amour qui créera alors et non plus moi. S'abîmer. Se démembrer. S'anéantir dans l'accomplissement et la passion de la vérité."[31]

---

shrink himself to a self that is 'condemned to be free.' To this shrunken or contracted self . . . God is dead, the past is dead, the present is the flight from the self's non-essential facticity toward being what it is not, the future is the field of possibles among which the self must choose its project of being beyond mere facticity, and freedom is the necessity of making a choice that will determine the self's own being. The freedom of the contracted self is the self's damnation not to be able not to be free" (111).

30. Quoted in Voegelin, *Anamnesis*, 370. Compare Edouard Altschul's description of the sickness—a "habitual nausea"—and the concomitant compulsive behavior that he has observed in Frankfort to Geyrenhoff. Doderer, *The Demons*, 1146–48.

31. Voegelin quotes this passage from Camus in French, the translation of which is then inserted by the editor and translator in brackets. To avoid confusion, I include the English translation here: "Not morality, but fulfillment. And there is no fulfillment other than that of love, meaning the renunciation of self and dying to the world. Going to the end. *To disappear.* To dissolve oneself in love. It will then be the power of love that will create, rather than myself. To lose oneself. To dismember oneself. To obliterate oneself in the fulfillment and the passion of truth" (Voegelin, *Anamnesis*, 371).

Camus thus recognized that love is the crucial element of human community—a love that extends to the community of Being; for without the latter, there is no human community.

That Geyrenhoff—who has been "revised," who has fallen from his hobbyhorse, who has fallen in love with Friederike—has returned to life and the community of man is confirmed by two reminders that "die Tiefe ist aussen" on the day that the Palace of Justice was burned. Geyrenhoff is visiting Gürtzner-Gontard, who as an outsider had earlier revealed truths about members of *die Unsrigen* that combined with other events occurring in first reality to derail Geyrenhoff's chronicling. They are watching the demonstration at the palace from Gürtzner-Gontard's window. While watching, they witness the death of a member of *die Unsrigen,* Imre Gyurkicz. Gyurkicz's death presents itself as another reminder that the depth is outside, for it is only with Gyurkicz's death that Geyrenhoff recognizes his kinship with Imre—with the fantasy of Imre's second reality, as well as Imre's reentry into the depth of reality as his "false bottom" bursts beneath him in death. Only with Imre's death does Geyrenhoff fully understand his own disillusionments and rejoin the human community, in which he can now call Imre his friend. Until his death, however, Gyurkicz has been an enigma to Geyrenhoff, for he had used the trappings in his room—a big pistol, a steel helmet, a human skull—as emblems of whatever role he was playing in any given situation. Moments before he is shot, Geyrenhoff, looking down on him, observes that

> he was using the big pistol I had seen in his room—one of his emblems. . . . An emblem suddenly finding employment, plunging into the thick of utility. It gave me a profound scare. . . . Metaphors were crashing to the ground, emblems breaking through their false bottoms into reality. It could not help happening—to Gyurkicz too. Every such consistently played fantasy sooner or later explodes into life. (*Ds,* 1233)

> It seemed to me in those clairvoyant seconds that Imre had been killed not by bullets but by the high-tension current of life itself, in which he had created a short-circuit. It is impossible to equip and adorn an inner surface, a false bottom, with many emblems over a period of years and then use one of the emblems to shatter it. The sudden contact with naked reality is fatal. Time-honored lies which play their necessary part in the economy of the psyche cannot suddenly be replaced by truth. Every second reality that is abruptly displaced by first reality leads to death.

Here, however, sheer pose had been transformed from the shadow to the substance of real bearing. I was with him entirely; it was as if I were inside him; I thought of the old song, "I had a comrade . . ." Truly, a part of myself fell to the pavement with him. Those seconds were the actual result of my chronicling. What I had just seen, and still saw, was the whole fruit of Imre's life. And it was good, it was sublime, even though he had harvested it only by his death. It was the restoration of his honor, the healing of his deepest injury, the elimination of his most secret shame. (*Ds,* 1233–34)

Geyrenhoff thinks that all of his chronicling—*"primum scribere deinde vivere"* (Write first, then live)—had led to that moment. Quickly, however, his initial thought is replaced by the idea that "the true fruit of my chronicling is Friederike." Geyrenhoff, however, remembers that

today, when everything is in every sense over, I know different. My first thought had been true. Of all those who had known the man lying dead down there, perhaps still clutching his emblem (I could not see this too plainly), I was probably the only one who understood him, who grasped the honorableness of his miserable death, who was with him now. For that, and for no other end, I had begun my scribblings and learned from them, been shipwrecked in the course of them. *Primum scribere deinde vivere.*

I turned away. Gürtzner, too, who was looking out, gazed gravely down at the dead man. "He was a friend of mine," I said—for only now could I really say that. I laid the field glasses on the window sill. (*Ds,* 1234)

When reality is contracted to the second reality of an autonomous self, an autonomous self that then attempts to create not only a reality for itself but also attempts to ground itself in its own depth—the depth of a false bottom—a confrontation with first reality by the emblems of the autonomously created self results in a breaking through the false bottom of the self into the true depth. Conversely, the true depth explodes the artificially constructed false ground of the self's second reality, which in Imre's case led to his death. Out of the depth in which the human being who lives in openness to his humanity, who recognizes his existence as a mortal-immortal in the *metaxy,* and who participates in the depth that encompasses it in the community of Being, arises Geyrenhoff's love for Imre von Gyurkicz as a fellow human being, as a friend.

"He was a friend of mine," I said. . . .

"*Oremus,*" Gürtzner answered and added the first two versicles of the *De Profundis.*[32] (*Ds,* 1234)

*Out of the depths have I cried unto thee, O Lord.*
*Lord, hear my voice; let thine ears be attentive to the voice of my supplications.*

I fell in at the third ("*si iniquitates observaveris, Domine: Domine, quis sustinebit?*").[33]

*But **there is** forgiveness with thee, that thou mayest be feared.*
*I wait for the Lord, my soul doth wait, and in his word do I hope.*
*My soul **waiteth** for the Lord more than they that watch for the morning: I say, **more than** they that watch for the morning.*
*Let Israel hope in the Lord: for with the Lord **there is** mercy, and with him **is** plenteous redemption.*
*And he shall redeem Israel from all his iniquities.*[34]

After the last shots it had grown quieter in the square down below. Shortly after we finished the prayer, the noon bells began to ring. I felt profound astonishment at the cold way these symbols of daily order seemed to comment on the scene. (*Ds,* 1234–35)

Out of the depths cries the soul for mercy and redemption.
*Malignitati falsa species libertatis inest.*

---

32. "Out of the depths." Psalm 130, used in the Roman Catholic burial service.
33. "If thou, Lord, shouldest mark iniquities, O Lord, who shall stand?"
34. Authorized King James Version.

# 6

## Novel of Divine Presence

### Flannery O'Connor's *The Violent Bear It Away*

The flux [of divine presence] has the structure of a divine-human encounter; every phase is an event of man's responding, or refusing to respond, to the presence of the divine ordering appeal. The consciousness of divine presence as the formative appeal endows every such event with the indelible character of a "present."

~ Eric Voegelin, "Wisdom and the Magic of the Extreme: A Meditation"

Lord, I believe; help thou mine unbelief.                    ~ Mark 9:24

---

W hen Flannery O'Connor died in 1964 at the age of 39, she left two novels, twenty-nine short stories, numerous essays, speeches, and interviews, and close to 800 letters.[1] Many readers find O'Connor's work archaically strange. It is, and moreover was, intended to be thus, for as she writes in her essay "The Nature and Aim of Fiction," "fiction should be both canny and uncanny."[2] All her stories emerged from her vocation as an artist-storyteller and Roman Catholic who lived in what Ralph Wood has called "the Christ-Haunted South." I intend here neither to justify O'Connor's work as a Catholic writer nor to explore her personal relation to the "Christ-Haunted South" in which she

---

1. While only 259 letters are included in her *Collected Works,* almost 800 were published in an earlier collection of her letters, *The Habit of Being,* ed. Fitzgerald.
2. O'Connor, "Nature and Aim of Fiction," 79.

lived and from which she drew the inspiration for, and the vernacular of, her stories. But neither will I ignore the central role that Christian faith plays in her writing, since to do so would be missing the point of her work. What I propose instead is to explore the ways in which the novel *The Violent Bear It Away*[3] captures and evokes the experience of mystery that O'Connor intended to embody in the story. *The Violent Bear It Away*, written from within the differentiations in consciousness effected by Greek philosophy and Christian revelation, exemplifies Being (the timeless) that has entered time, i.e., the Time of the Tale.

## THEORETICAL CONGRUENCE: O'CONNOR AND VOEGELIN

Because there exist striking parallels between the philosopher Eric Voegelin and the storyteller Flannery O'Connor, I will first focus on the theoretical principles that O'Connor expressed in her prose writings and letters before I approach the novel itself. This is a departure from my procedure elsewhere, since for the most part I have avoided the novelists' own theoretical statements about their work. While this departure may appear to diverge from the approach to novels that I have advocated in chapter 3, my response to *The Violent Bear It Away* still relies upon an imaginative-cognitive reading followed by meditation so that the symbolization is permitted to elicit the experiential complex that the novel enacts. Reenactment, as we will see, is not inconsistent with O'Connor's understanding of the nature and purpose of fiction. Moreover, the reenactment that I recommend is rooted in both Voegelin's and O'Connor's understanding that the truth of art is evocative. I again remind the reader that what I have written and am writing about literature, philosophy, and reading only points back to the novels themselves. Reenactment can only happen in the consciousness of an individual who invites evocation to occur. Experiencing the novel is the first step toward reenactment. In the case of an O'Connor novel, this experience almost always begins as a jarring confrontation with the reader's sensibilities. The novel then becomes the way back into the experience that gave birth to the novel originally. For O'Connor, the experience of mystery that the novel elicits leads the reader deeper into

3. O'Connor, *The Violent Bear It Away*, in *Three by Flannery O'Connor*. Although all page references are to this edition of *The Violent Bear It Away*, I have checked the editorial accuracy of selected passages against O'Connor, *Collected Works*. I should note that *The Violent Bear It Away* was originally published in 1960.

reality and the mystery of existence. She writes that "the type of mind that can understand good fiction is not necessarily the educated mind, but it is at all times the kind of mind that is willing to have its sense of mystery deepened by contact with reality, and its sense of reality deepened by contact with mystery."[4] Of course, reenactment rooted in readings structured by imaginative-cognitive-meditative participation can only occur because of the "circumstanced equality"[5] of all human beings, i.e., because human beings exist in the *metaxy* as participants in the reality of the community of Being.

O'Connor's aesthetic and theoretical principles and concerns converge with the broader philosophical work of Voegelin in several areas. Both thinkers observe in the modern world a "loss" of reality and call for either a return to reality (O'Connor) or a recapturing of reality (Voegelin). Both thinkers understand *reality* to mean something more than the visible-sensible world. Both thinkers recognize that at the core of reality there exists a fundamental and impenetrable mystery. Both thinkers emphasize that human experiences of what O'Connor calls the "invisible world" and what Voegelin calls "non-existent reality" are expressed in imaginative linguistic symbolizations. I will focus on these points of agreement.

O'Connor often uses violent episodes in her stories, and consequently her stories have many times been characterized as too dark or too strange. In commenting on the use of violence in her story "The Misfit," she wrote that

> in my own stories I have found that violence is strangely capable of returning my characters to reality and preparing them to accept their moment of grace. Their heads are so hard that almost nothing else will do the work. This idea, that reality is something to which we must be returned at considerable cost, is one which is seldom understood by the casual reader, but it is one which is implicit in the Christian view of the world.[6]

Her call for a return to reality relies, of course, upon the Christian vision of reality, which includes more than the visible-material world, the belief that human beings are more than their bodies, and that

---

4. O'Connor, "Nature and Aim of Fiction," 79. Thus openness to reality and its mystery is a necessary prerequisite to "understanding" an O'Connor story.

5. Cf. chapter 2 above for discussion of "circumstanced equality."

6. O'Connor, "On Her Own Work," 112.

human consciousness is more than a biochemical accident. Thus the call for a return to reality is an invitation to her readers to recognize that insofar as they ignore or deny this more-than-material reality they have become alienated from the true source of their humanity, of their human being-ness as *imago Dei.*

Voegelin's call to recapture reality is rooted, we will recall, in the experience of economic, political, social, and spiritual disorder that led him to search for the source of order. As Voegelin discovered in his historical search of order, the experience of social and political disorder has led human beings throughout time to search for and experience an order in the cosmos that is deeper than the experienced disorder of their own times. But even after the articulations of experiential discoveries of an invisible reality behind the visible (or, in Voegelin's terms, of a nonexistent divine reality behind existent reality), the burden of the material-visible reality is perceived to be so great or, as in the modern era, the sciences of the natural world are so successful, that some have chosen to deny the reality of the invisible, except perhaps as rarified extensions of the visible. Love, for example, would thus be understood as the result of biochemistry. Others have denied the invisible simply because it would remind them that there exists a reality greater than themselves, which resists attempts to control it. Still others have resorted to Doderer's *Apperzeptions-Verweigerung* (the refusal to apperceive the reality to which their own composite nature grants them access), designating themselves as the source of their own order and meaning.[7] Finally, others simply live as though the invisible reality does not exist, thereby denying their basic humanity. Even material disorder—such as war or genocide or economic exploitation—and denial, however, must be recognized as manifestations of reality. Thus, Voegelin calls for a recapturing of reality from those who would appear to deform the invisible reality but who are only deforming their capacity and ability and will to understand and love the nonexistent divine ground as the source of order. In *Autobiographical Reflections,* Voegelin succinctly outlines what it means to recapture reality: "Recapturing reality in opposition to its contemporary deformation requires a considerable amount of work. One has to reconstruct the fundamental categories of existence, experience, consciousness, and reality."[8] In O'Connor's

7. As we will see below, the character Rayber Tarwater in *The Violent Bear It Away* denies the divinely ordering reality and deforms his life in the belief that as a human being with human dignity it is within his power to create his own meaning and order.
8. Voegelin, *Autobiographical Reflections,* 96.

stories, the fundamental philosophical categories of existence, experience, consciousness, and reality are transposed/transformed into literary expressions: characters engaged in the struggle to respond to or deny the divine ordering reality. While Hungarian novelist Péter Nádas observes that all novels wade "through lived experience,"[9] O'Connor reaches in her own fiction for "the concrete expression of mystery—mystery that is lived."[10]

What is this reality to which O'Connor recalls her characters and to which we as human beings "must be returned at considerable cost"? Since O'Connor is neither a theologian nor a philosopher, she is not concerned to articulate her experiences and understanding of reality, except as they concern her vocation as a storyteller. So while she addresses the importance of a writer's view of reality for the fiction that she writes, ultimately she intends that her vision of reality, governed by Christian belief and Catholic dogma, will emerge from her stories. Therefore, whenever she refers to reality in her prose writings or letters, the references are almost always made in the context of her view of the nature of fiction. For example, she clarifies the simple declaration made in a letter to Elizabeth Hester that "the visible universe is a reflection of the invisible universe"[11] in her essay "Some Aspects of the Grotesque in Southern Fiction." There she asserts, "All novelists are fundamentally seekers and describers of the real, but the realism of each novelist will depend on his view of the ultimate reaches of reality."[12] And what are the "ultimate reaches of reality" for O'Connor? If we read the following statement in conjunction with her declaration that in her case Christian "belief . . . is the engine that makes perception operate,"[13] her understanding of the "ultimate reaches of reality" becomes clearer. In "Novelist and Believer," she asserts that

> it makes a great difference to the look of a novel whether its author believes that the world came late into being and continues to come by a creative act of God, or whether he believes that the world and ourselves are the product of a cosmic accident. It makes a great difference to his novel whether he believes that we are created in God's image, or whether he

---

9. Péter Nádas, "The Novelist and His Selfs," 18.
10. O'Connor to Eileen Hall, March 10, 1956, in O'Connor, *Habit,* 144.
11. O'Connor to Elizabeth Hester, January 13, 1956, ibid., 128.
12. O'Connor, "Some Aspects of the Grotesque in Southern Fiction," 40–41.
13. O'Connor, "Her Own Work," 109.

believes we create God in our own. It makes a great difference whether he believes that our wills are free, or bound like those of the other animals.[14]

Of course, in each of these dichotomies, O'Connor identifies with the accepted Christian view, i.e., that the world exists by a creative act of God, that human beings are created in God's image, and that human beings are essentially free beings. At the core of the "ultimate reaches of reality" though, lying deeper than the Christian dogma, is the experience of mystery. And in O'Connor's fiction the experience of mystery drives her storytelling. In another passage, from "Some Aspects of the Grotesque in Southern Fiction," she addresses the consequences for fiction writing of the belief in the mystery that lies at the depth of the "ultimate reaches of reality."

> If the writer believes that our life is and will remain essentially mysterious, if he looks upon us as beings existing in a created order to whose laws we freely respond, then what he sees on the *surface* will be of interest to him only as he can *go through it into an experience of mystery itself.* His kind of fiction will always be pushing its own limits outward toward the limits of *mystery,* because for this kind of writer, the meaning of a story does not begin except at a depth where adequate motivation and adequate psychology and the various determinations have been exhausted. Such a writer will be interested in what we don't understand rather than in what we do. He will be interested in possibility rather than in probability. He will be interested in characters who are forced out to meet evil and grace and who act on a trust beyond themselves—whether they know very clearly what it is they act upon or not. To the modern mind, this kind of character, and his creator, are typical Don Quixotes, tilting at what is not there.[15]

O'Connor's focus on mystery has the distinct quality of the recognition of creatureliness, of having been created and of existing in a world that is divinely created. This focus connects O'Connor's work with what Voegelin calls the primary experience of the cosmos, which characterizes the literary form of myth found in cosmological societies and civilizations before the leap in being or the differentiation in human understanding of the cosmos into the divine-transcendent and the worldly-immanent. Voegelin, in his later work, explains that even after differentiation of the cosmos into transcendent and immanent, viable

14. O'Connor, "Novelist and Believer," 156–57.
15. O'Connor, "Grotesque in Southern Fiction," 41–42. Emphasis added.

philosophical thought must build upon that primary experience of the cosmos; for without it, philosophical symbolizations are experientially ungrounded. He expresses this in the assertion that "the cosmos does not go away" simply because of a differentiation in our understanding of ourselves as human beings. As a philosopher, Voegelin sought to understand and articulate through his imaginative-cognitive talents the truth of existence. All that the philosopher can do is to give voice to his experiences of reality insofar as these experiences can be symbolized. But ultimately, even the philosopher's love of the ground of his being must yield to the recognition that, as Voegelin writes in his last work, "the epiphany of structures in reality—be they atoms, molecules, genes, biological species, races, human consciousness, or language—is a mystery inaccessible to explanation."[16] The philosopher, as representative for all human beings, asks as Leibniz does, Why is there something, why not nothing? and Why is the something as it is and not different?; but these questions cannot alter the impenetrable mystery of *metaxy*, of the "mortal-immortal" human being. The recognition of mystery is an important component of philosophical wisdom, as Glenn Hughes asserts:

> The mysteries about which Voegelin writes are depths of meaning whose hiddenness is apparent, and which could be known fully only if reality as a whole were known, while the human knower remains a participant in reality with a limited perspective, unable to fully penetrate the meanings that constitute human existence.[17]

Just because a fiction writer is interested in mystery, O'Connor maintained, does not mean that she is able to dispense with the visible, concrete world. "I would not like to suggest," she said, "that this kind of writer, because his interest is predominantly in mystery, is able in any sense to slight the concrete. Fiction begins where human knowledge begins—with the senses—and every fiction writer is bound by this fundamental aspect of his medium."[18] Like Joseph Conrad, whose work she

16. Voegelin, *In Search of Order*, 31.

17. Hughes, *Mystery and Myth*, 2. In the "Voegelin Glossary," Sandoz defines *mystery*: "Mystery is knowable only through participation and by way of analogical symbols or myth" (Voegelin, *Autobiographical Reflections*, ed. Sandoz, 168–69). While mystery is knowable through participation, it cannot didactically be encapsulated in the intentionalist language of the external world but only symbolized in myth—story—and through analogical language in philosophy. Hence the necessity of the imaginative reenactment of literary symbolizations.

18. O'Connor, "Grotesque in Southern Fiction," 42.

admired, O'Connor was committed to rendering the "highest possible justice to the visible world," for only through the observable world of the senses could the invisible world and its mystery be accessed. Only by embodying in her stories the "concrete world in order to find at its depths the image of its source, the image of ultimate reality,"[19] could O'Connor begin to express her conviction that "the whole story is the meaning, because it is an experience, not an abstraction."[20] Like Dostoyevsky, O'Connor expected that the reader will be "drawn into the cast of characters in real existential dramas structured by the twin abysses of experience—the underground of nature and the divine ground of being—as apprehended through all the modalities of thought and passion."[21]

In addition to emphasizing the expression of the mystery of the depths of ultimate reality through the replication in language of the concrete, visible world, O'Connor aspired to the creation in her stories of a wholeness of vision that also expressed mystery. John F. Desmond observes that "probably more than any other American writer of her generation, she managed to create a coherent wholeness of vision and form."[22] The coherence of O'Connor's stories issues from two sources: (1) a technical commitment to the idea that the form of a story emerges from the content of the story (hence the meaning cannot be divorced from the story itself), and (2) her belief in a divine creation. In "The Nature and Aim of Fiction" she wrote that "in the best stories [technique] is something organic, something that grows out of the material, and this being the case, it is different for every story of any account that has ever been written."[23] In the same essay she wrote: "The longer you look at one object, the more of the world you see in it; and it's well to

19. O'Connor, "Novelist and Believer," 157.
20. O'Connor, "Nature and Aim of Fiction," 73.
21. Sandoz, *Political Apocalypse*, 276.
22. Desmond, *Risen Sons: Flannery O'Connor's Vision of History,* 12.
23. O'Connor, "Nature and Aim of Fiction," 67. Cf. Voegelin's statement to Heilman (cited throughout our text): "Underlying all later, differentiated forms, however, there remains the basic Tale which expresses Being in flux. Time, then, would not be an empty container into which you can fill any content, but there would be as many times as there are types of differentiated content. . . . This reflexion would lead into a philosophy of language, in which the basic Tale would appear as the instrument of man's dealing with reality through language—and adequately at that. Form and content, thus, would be inseparable: The Tale, if it is any good, has to deal with Being in flux, however much differentiated the insights into the complex structures of reality may be" (Voegelin to Heilman, August, 13, 1964, in *AFIL,* letter 103, p. 223).

remember that the serious fiction writer always writes about the whole world, no matter how limited his particular scene."[24]

Her belief that the meaning of a story is fully embodied in the story itself arose from her conviction that observable reality is not just a creation but a continuing manifestation of divine-invisible reality, and that through her creative efforts she could evoke divine-invisible reality via the linguistic rendering of concrete-visible reality. To accomplish this, O'Connor argued, the storyteller relies upon a "prophetic vision" that interacts with the imaginative faculty of man and makes the fiction writer "a realist of distances." She believed that only this prophetic realism produces great novels. Moreover, she asserted that this vision, characteristic of the fiction writer, "does not hesitate to distort appearances in order to show a hidden truth."[25] While this prophetic vision may be a personal imaginative gift possessed by the writer—O'Connor certainly believed that she was given the gift of writing[26]—vision in her own case was "lengthened" by the church. "For the Catholic novelist," she declared, "the prophetic vision is not simply a matter of his personal imaginative gift; it is also a matter of the Church's gift, which, unlike his own, is safeguarded and deals with greater matters. It is one of the functions of the Church to transmit the prophetic vision that is good for all time, and when the novelist has this as a part of his own vision, he has a powerful extension of sight."[27] Elsewhere she called the faculty of a fiction writer to deepen the meaning of his story "anagogical vision," which, she clarified,

> is the kind of vision that is able to see different levels of reality in one image or one situation. The medieval commentators on Scripture found three kinds of meaning in the literal level of the sacred text: one they called allegorical, in which one fact pointed to another; one they called tropological, or moral, which had to do with what should be done; and one they called anagogical, which had to do with the *Divine life and our*

---

24. O'Connor, "Nature and Aim of Fiction," 77.
25. O'Connor, "Catholic Novelists and Their Readers," 179.
26. In "The Nature and Aim of Fiction," she said: "Last spring I talked here, and one of the girls asked me, 'Miss O'Connor, why do you write?' and I said, 'Because I'm good at it,' and at once I felt a considerable disapproval in the atmosphere." She went on to say that "there is no excuse for anyone to write fiction for public consumption unless he has been called to do so by the presence of a gift.... A gift of any kind is a considerable responsibility. It is a mystery in itself, something gratuitous and wholly undeserved, something whose real uses will probably always be hidden from us" (81).
27. O'Connor, "Catholic Novelists and Their Readers," 179–80.

*participation in it.* Although this was a method applied to biblical exegesis, it was also an attitude toward all of creation, and a way of reading nature which included most possibilities, and I think it is this enlarged view of the human scene that the fiction writer has to cultivate if he is ever going to write stories that have any chance of becoming a permanent part of our literature.[28]

The embodiment of invisible reality in an art dependent upon a faithful reflection of the material world was for O'Connor an incarnational act. Rooted deeply in her Christian faith, her fiction expressed through the Tale the historical Incarnation of the Divine. Desmond argues that since she believed her fiction to be incarnational, the medieval doctrine of the analogy of being, or *analogia entis,* was "central to her aesthetic because it gave a philosophical foundation to the kind of typological fiction she aimed to write—with one action conveying several layers of meaning. But most important, it provided a coherent unity between her technique and her vision of history—between fictional incarnation and *the* Incarnation—and thus, I believe, enabled her to create that unique wholeness which is such a distinctive feature of her work."[29]

To the extent that Flannery's vocation as an artist seeks to "penetrate the concrete world in order to find at its depths the image of its source, the image of ultimate reality," her work is an aesthetic complement to the philosophical vocation of Voegelin: to recapture an understanding of nonexistent, divine reality as a ground and source of meaning and order in the visible world. Furthermore, O'Connor's view that her own stories arise from her belief in a divine creation and the *parousia* of the divine in time, the Incarnation, parallels Voegelin's philosophical quest that proceeds from "the divine kinesis" that moved him to seek the divine ground of his being as well as his quest understood as a *fides quaerens intellectum.*

28. O'Connor, "The Nature and Aim of Fiction," 72–73. Emphasis added.
29. Desmond, *Risen Sons,* 31. God, according to the medieval doctrine of *analogia entis,* is "radically transcendent Being Itself (Aquinas's *Ipsum Esse Subsistens*), in which all particular entities or existents exist by 'participation.' Implies that the only adequate language for transcendent reality is analogical and that the relative adequacy of such language is grounded in the inherently analogical character of all participated being" (Sandoz, "Voegelin Glossary," in *Autobiographical Reflections,* 150).

## THE VIOLENT BEAR IT AWAY

In introductory remarks that prefaced her reading of the story "A Good Man Is Hard to Find," O'Connor asserted that "a story really isn't any good unless it successfully resists paraphrase, unless it hangs on and expands the mind. Properly, you analyze to enjoy, but it's equally true that to analyze with any discrimination, you have to have enjoyed already."[30] Despite the fact that *The Violent Bear It Away* resists paraphrase both of form and content (I will discuss the reasons for this resistance below), I must at least indicate through a very general summary the content of the story.

### THE VIOLENT BEAR IT AWAY: AN OVERVIEW

The primary focus of the story is a fourteen-year-old boy, Francis Marion Tarwater (called Tarwater in the narrative), whose destiny—made clear in the story—is to be a prophet. Tarwater had been baptized and kidnapped to be raised up for his prophetic vocation by his great-uncle Mason Tarwater (referred to as Old Tarwater), also a prophet of the Lord: "I brought you out here to raise you a Christian, and more than a Christian, a prophet!" (*TVBIA*, 132). Tarwater and his great-uncle live deep in the woods, on Old Tarwater's subsistence farm called Powderhead, where the old man also makes moonshine. The story opens immediately following the death of Old Tarwater, whose aim in life had been to baptize his grandnephew Bishop, the retarded son of his nephew Rayber Tarwater. Before he died, Old Tarwater had instructed Tarwater to bury him on the place and erect a cross above him; then Tarwater was to baptize Bishop. "'If by the time I die,' he said to Tarwater, 'I haven't got him baptized, it'll be up to you. It'll be the first mission the Lord sends you'" (*TVBIA*, 128). Since Old Tarwater failed to baptize Bishop, the task falls to Tarwater. Tarwater seeks to avoid his great-uncle's instructions first by getting drunk and burning the cabin in which they had lived (thinking that the old man's body was still there) and then by going to the city, where Bishop and Rayber live, in order to confront and deny his vocation to baptize Bishop. Tarwater's struggle to deny his vocation to baptize Bishop and to become a prophet supplies the tension and focus of the story. The devil appearing to Tarwater in the form of his alter ego,

30. O'Connor, "Her Own Work," 108.

first as a stranger and then as a friend whose voice mimics his own, and Rayber, who had himself been kidnapped, baptized, and instructed by Old Tarwater, bolster Tarwater's intention to become free by denying his destiny. Baptism is the central thematic focus of the story—the baptisms of Rayber when he was seven and Tarwater as a baby by Old Tarwater, and the baptism-to-come of Bishop by Tarwater. At some mysterious level these baptisms define the vocations and responses to the divine appeal of Tarwater and Rayber.

It is clear that Tarwater is aware of his vocation as a prophet, because he expected his call to come in the dramatic ways that Old Testament figures like Daniel, Moses, or Joshua had been spoken to by God. Moreover, not only had he been baptized by Old Tarwater, but he had also been educated by the old man in "Figures, Reading, Writing, and History beginning with Adam expelled from the Garden and going on down through the presidents to Herbert Hoover and on in speculation toward the Second Coming and the Day of Judgment" (*TVBIA*, 125). Finally, Old Tarwater "had schooled him in the evils that befall prophets; in those that come from the world, which are trifling, and those that come from the Lord and burn the prophet clean; for he himself had been burned clean and burned clean again" (*TVBIA*, 126).

Rayber, a schoolteacher who has spent his life rejecting his baptism by Old Tarwater and his own call to a religious vocation, plays a crucial role in the story by trying to convince Tarwater that every man's salvation is in his own hands. We learn that the old man had once recounted to Tarwater that Rayber had rejected in the name of human dignity his attempt to baptize Bishop. Rayber had asserted that Bishop would be "brought up to live in the real world" and to expect only what he could do for himself. "He's going to be his own saviour. He's going to be free" (*TVBIA*, 165). As to his own destiny, Rayber had said to Old Tarwater: "I've straightened the tangle you made. Straightened it by pure will power. I've made myself straight" (*TVBIA*, 166).

Tarwater's struggle to deny his vocation results in his drowning Bishop, whom Rayber had earlier attempted, and failed, to drown. As Tarwater is drowning Bishop he involuntarily speaks the words of baptism, thereby failing to avoid his destiny. After the drowning of Bishop, Tarwater hitches a ride with a stranger in a "lavender and cream-colored car," who gives him drugged whiskey, takes him into the woods, rapes him, and leaves him alone, unconscious in the woods. When Tarwater comes to himself, "his expression seemed to contract until it reached some point beyond rage or pain. Then a loud dry cry tore out of him and his mouth fell back into place" (*TVBIA*, 261). He lights a pine bough, burns the site of the rape, and trudges off to Powderhead, where he discovers that Buford Munson, a Negro who had come to get a jug of moonshine right after Old Tarwater had died, had in fact taken on Tarwater's job of burying the old man and had erected a cross above his grave.

Then, in a vision of Old Tarwater finding his place among the multitude to be fed on the bread of life, Tarwater sees "a red-gold tree of fire," the same fire that had appeared to Daniel, Elijah, and Moses. "He threw himself to the ground and with his face against the dirt of the grave, he heard the command. GO WARN THE CHILDREN OF GOD OF THE TERRIBLE SPEED OF MERCY. The words were as silent as seeds opening one at a time in his blood" (*TVBIA*, 267). The novel ends with Tarwater smearing dirt from his great-uncle's grave onto his forehead and setting off "toward the dark city, where the children of God lay sleeping" (*TVBIA*, 267).

### READING *THE VIOLENT BEAR IT AWAY*

My comments on *The Violent Bear It Away* are based upon reenactment (discussed in chapter 3). Consequently, my understanding of the novel and what I will say about it grew over time as I proceeded through the stages of a first reading, an analytical reading, reflection, and finally a synthetic rereading. When I begin the third sentence of the next paragraph with "The first indication that *The Violent Bear It Away* is a myth or cosmion . . . ," one must understand that my "first indication" did not necessarily arise nor was it evoked immediately upon the initial reading.

*The Violent Bear It Away* is a cosmion, defined by Voegelin as "a reflection of the unity of the cosmos as a whole," and like a cosmion it is "some sort of myth." Voegelin observed that the problem in art is "how to produce such units and make them convincing models of the unity of the world."[31] The first indication that *The Violent Bear It Away* is a myth or cosmion that reflects "the unity of the cosmos as a whole" comes as one attempts to place the characters and events of the novel in space and time. While the physical setting of the story is realistic—the events of the story happen on a farm deep in the woods, at a rural "lake resort," and in a city with residential areas possessing the material

---

31. Voegelin, "In Search of the Ground," 240.

*accoutrements* of modernity like roads, automobiles, lawyers' offices, restaurants, boat rentals, and so on—these places and things are not named. Their realism derives from the attention that O'Connor gives to the material, visible details of place and things. Consequently, the reader is projected or invited into a place that seems real but unplaceable geographically. About all the reader can say regarding the setting is that the story takes place in the rural American South. But this statement itself derives primarily from external knowledge—about the South and about Flannery O'Connor and her commitment to the region of her birth and residence—that the reader brings to the story.

With regard to the time of the story, the reader is also left in the dark. Of course, the reader can infer a general time frame from the descriptions of events and places or even from the fact that Tarwater was educated in history "beginning with Adam expelled from the Garden and going on down through the presidents to Herbert Hoover and on in speculation toward the Second Coming and the Day of Judgment." The initial phrase grounds man's existence in the divine creation; the middle phrase, "going down through the presidents to Herbert Hoover," brings the reader up to the Great Depression; and the final phrase projects the reader out of time and into the timeless. From the chronology of Tarwater's history lesson we understand that the existential time of humanity is flanked by the "time" of the beginning in creation and the "time" of the ending of time in the Beyond. This "time" of the Beginning and of the Beyond is the "time that is out of time" of the "Time of the Tale." We also understand that this time that is flanked by the timelessness of Beginning and Beyond is the time of the *metaxy,* the In-Between of man's existence as mortal-immortal. The reader more than anything else "senses" the wholeness and unity of the story through the placeless rootedness in space and the timeless rootedness in time.

Locating the story in a place out of space and a time out of time in this way enabled O'Connor to draw the reader into the *metaxic* structure of the story; that is, the real place and time in which the story occurs is the consciousness, the *metaxy,* of the mortal-immortal reader. In O'Connor's terms, this location technique enabled her to unify form and content so that the story itself is the meaning and so that the reenactment of the story becomes the experience of meaning. When this wholeness of the placeless and timeless nature of the story envelopes the reader, the analytical distinction between the story and its meaning disappears. One no longer needs to ask "What is the meaning of this story?" because the meaning has mysteriously been delivered as the story—like the silent seeds blooming in Tarwater's blood—blossoms in the consciousness of the reader.

The second indication that the story has a mythical wholeness derives from the cognitive-imaginative excitement that it generates in the consciousness of the reader. The only term that I can find to describe how the components of the story (plot, character, actions, occurrences) collectively result in this excitement is that they are *charged*. This "chargedness" of the story signifies both an emotional loading (analogous to loading an explosive charge for a gun) and an electrical charging (analogous to the charging of a battery) and is communicated to the reader by the narrative/literary compactness of a story from which, according to O'Connor, not one word could be stricken. While I only dimly perceived or intuited this excitement on the first reading, it fully emerged into my consciousness during the synthetic rereading of the story itself. I do not fully understand how O'Connor accomplished this, but that she intended to implant an emotional impact in her story is beyond doubt. In a lecture at Sweetbriar College, delivered in 1963, she said:

> When I write a novel in which the central action is a baptism, I am very well aware that for a majority of my readers, baptism is a meaningless rite, and so in my novel I have to see that this baptism carries enough awe and mystery to jar the reader into some kind of emotional recognition of its significance. To this end I have to bend the whole novel—its language, its structure, its action. *I have to make the reader feel, in his bones if nowhere else, that something is going on here that counts.* Distortion in this case is an instrument; exaggeration has a purpose, and the whole structure of the story or novel has been made what it is because of belief. This is not the kind of distortion that destroys; it is the kind that reveals, or should reveal.[32]

Certainly one indication of this "chargedness" is her description of Tarwater's relation to all of creation and material reality. Very early in the story, Tarwater remembers that Old Tarwater preached to him that "Jesus is the bread of life," and he asks himself: "Had the bush flamed for Moses, the sun stood still for Joshua, the lions turned aside before Daniel only to prophesy the bread of life? Jesus? He felt a terrible disappointment in that conclusion, a dread that it was true" (*TVBIA*, 135). Even more, he feared that this conclusion lay at the heart of his great-

---

32. O'Connor, "Novelist and Believer," 162. Emphasis added.

uncle's "madness, this hunger" and that it might be passed down to him in his blood, only to strike him one day with the same hunger. In order to avoid these thoughts and conclusions, Tarwater tried to keep his perception of the world around him shallow, for the world and creation itself carried, he feared, the truth of the old man's beliefs.

> It was as if he were afraid that if he let his eye rest for an instant longer than was needed to place something—a spade, a hoe, the mule's hind quarters before his plow, the red furrow under him—that the thing would suddenly stand before him, strange and terrifying, demanding that he name it and name it justly and be judged for the name he gave it. He did all he could to avoid this threatened intimacy of creation. When the Lord's call came, he wished it to be a voice from out of a clear and empty sky, the trumpet of the Lord God Almighty, untouched by any fleshly hand or breath. He expected to see wheels of fire in the eyes of unearthly beasts.[33] (*TVBIA*, 136)

Creation itself stands as a visible sign of the divine presence that Tarwater must not recognize for fear that he would have to affirm the truth of the old man's faith.

Bishop also stands as a visible sign of divine presence. And just as Tarwater fears recognizing the material creation if he looks too closely, he also fears looking at Bishop; he "never looked lower than the top of his head except by accident for the silent country appeared to be reflected again in the center of his [Bishop's] eyes. It stretched out there, limitless and clear" (*TVBIA*, 218). From Bishop's eyes the silent *imago Dei* stares out as a rebuke to Tarwater's refusal of his calling and, simultaneously, as an invitation to accept it. Another instance, and a far more mysterious one, of this charged character of the narrative occurs when Tarwater baptizes Bishop, his retarded cousin, incident to his drowning; one senses in this double action an awe and mystery that is rationally inexplicable. It is in the violence of O'Connor's narrative "distortion" and "exaggeration" that the act reveals a mystery.

To explore further the "charged" characteristics of the story, I will refer once again to three passages from Voegelin's work: two from his explanation of the Time of the Tale in his August 13, 1964, letter to Heilman and the passage that I have chosen as the epigraph for this chapter. In the letter to Heilman he wrote:

33. Rayber too must suppress his apperception in favor of a shallow perception of the world around him, especially to his perception of Bishop, in order to deny what he experiences and knows to be true. See below.

The basic form of myth, the "tale" in the widest sense, including the epic as well as the dramatic account of happenings, has a specific time, immanent to the tale, whose specific character consists in the ability to combine human, cosmic and divine elements into one story. I have called it, already in *Order and History,* the Time of the Tale. It expresses the experience of being (that embraces all sorts of reality, the cosmos) in flux.

⚬⚬

The Tale, if it is any good, has to deal with Being in flux, however much differentiated the insights into the complex structures of reality may be. (*AFIL,* letter 103, August 13, 1964, p. 223)

In a later essay, "Wisdom and the Magic of the Extreme: A Meditation," he wrote that

the flux [of divine presence] has the structure of a divine-human encounter; every phase is an event of man's responding, or refusing to respond, to the presence of the divine ordering appeal. The consciousness of divine presence as the formative appeal endows every such event with the indelible character of a "present."[34]

The "charge" of awe and mystery with which O'Connor infuses *The Violent Bear It Away* manifests itself in the deft way that she combines "human, cosmic and divine elements in the story." And, as we have seen, any story that combines these three components will of necessity also be expressing in the art of the narrative the experience of Being in flux, or, as Voegelin also phrases it, the flux of divine presence.

The cosmic elements of O'Connor's novel mediate the flux of divine presence as this presence "reveals" itself to the characters of the story— especially to Tarwater and Rayber. Not only does O'Connor manage to express in language the divine appeal mediated by cosmic elements to Tarwater and Rayber, she also expresses the existential struggle that these characters endure in their freedom to respond, or not, to that appeal. Finally, their responses are structured: in the case of Tarwater, by his experiences of the Beginning and the Beyond, and in the case of Rayber, by his rejection of the reality of the appeal, which results in the deformation of his life. To these expressions of the divine appeal and to the existential responses of Tarwater and Rayber we now turn.

The combination of cosmic, divine, and human components characterizes a Tale that is mythical in nature, but to specify what these elements

---

34. Voegelin, "Wisdom and the Magic of the Extreme," 346.

are and how they combine to form a mythical tale is difficult. In reading the story, one "senses" or intuits this combination; and as one didactically attempts to identify this combination, the living tissue of the
story recedes into the background. Nevertheless one tries.[35] One of the
difficulties of specification arises from the interpenetration of the different elements in the story; but if we understand the cosmic element as
thing-reality, the divine element as the It-reality, and the human as the
*metaxy*, or In-Between reality, it becomes possible to specify and discuss
these components. The human component, consciousness, exists in the
*metaxy* because it participates *both* in thing-reality insofar as its locus is
the mortality of the body *and* in the encompassing It-reality insofar as
its locus is the immortality of the divine ground. The *metaxy* of human
consciousness is the spatio-metaphorical-ontological place where the
apperception of mortality—those things that come into existence and
must go out of existence—mingles with, interpenetrates, and participates in the apperception of the immortality and lastingness of the
timeless divine. Thus in talking about the combination of components
in *The Violent Bear It Away*, we emphasize the fact that the divine It-
reality that is mediated (even in the differentiated galaxy of O'Connor's
Christianity) by the cosmic thing-reality is experienced in the embodied consciousness of the human characters. Bearing in mind Voegelin's
emphasis on participation as central to understanding the human experience of reality will help us open O'Connor's story to reveal how the
combination of cosmic, divine, and human elements is achieved, for the
combination is rooted in the participation—especially of Tarwater's
consciousness—in the cosmic world around Tarwater and its envelop-
ment by the divine presence.

The actions of Tarwater and Rayber represent different responses to
"the divine ordering appeal," even though "the presence of the divine
ordering appeal" manifests It-self differently for each. Rayber personi-
fies, in his agony and his obstinacy, modern man in revolt against the
divine ground of his existence. In the story he embodies the deformed
man, the man who simultaneously apperceives but refuses his own
apperception—as Voegelin says is characteristic of Hegel or Marx.

---

35. For this reason it is important to have read cognitively-imaginatively-medita-
tively the story before attempting the specification. Therefore as one meditates on the
story *as* meaning, one relies upon *tacit knowing*, to use a term developed by the philosopher Michael Polanyi. The specific knowledge of the events and occurrences in the story
can only be understood against this tacit dimension of meaning. Cf. Polanyi, *The Tacit
Dimension*, 1–25.

Rayber is the man who knows, even experiences, the divine—his know-ing is in his blood and its manifestation is in the "undertow in his blood"—but who nonetheless denies the divine reality (*TVBIA*, 192). Not only does he experience the divine, he even recognizes his own vocation as originating in the divine ground, but he wills his denial in the name of the real world—the material world in which "what's dead stays that way"[36]—and the human dignity and freedom of autonomous man. "The great dignity of man," Rayber said to Tarwater, "is his ability to say: I am born once and no more. What I can see and do for myself and my fellowman in this life is all of my portion and I'm content with it. It's enough to be a man" (*TVBIA*, 225). Rayber believes that

> the affliction was in the family. It lay hidden in the line of blood that touched them, flowing from some ancient source, some desert prophet or polesitter, until, its power unabated, it appeared in the old man and him and, he surmised, in the boy. Those it touched were condemned to fight it constantly or be ruled by it. The old man had been ruled by it. He, at the cost of a full life, staved it off. What the boy would do hung in the balance. (*TVBIA*, 192–93)

Rayber shares with Tarwater the "affliction" passed down to both of them by Old Tarwater, and he understands that Tarwater's "compul-sion," as he calls it, is to baptize Bishop; but he says: "my own is more complicated, but the principle is the same. The way we have to fight it is the same" (*TVBIA*, 238). Rayber believes that the old man's legacy both to him and Tarwater was a psychological compulsion that must be fought. Without fighting his compulsion, a man cannot maintain the human dignity of autonomous man. But what is Rayber's "more com-plicated" compulsion, what is the nature of the divine appeal as it comes to him? Love. It is love, all-encompassing, all-embracing, uncondi-tional, mystical love that he rejects; and as with Tarwater's response to his fear of the intimacy of creation, Rayber struggles to maintain a shal-low perception of reality. He refused to look at anything too long, for anything—"a stick or a stone, the line of a shadow, the absurd old man's walk of a starling crossing the sidewalk"—could bring on "the love that terrified him" (*TVBIA*, 192). Through a rigid asceticism—refusing to look at anything too long, denying unnecessary sensual satisfactions, sleeping in a "narrow iron bed," working "in a straight-backed chair,"

---

36. O'Connor, *Wise Blood*, in *Three by Flannery O'Connor*, 54.

eating sparsely, speaking little, socializing with the dullest friends—
Rayber obstinately denied the divine pull of love.

> He was not afraid of love in general. He knew the value of it and how
> it could be used. He had seen it transform in cases where nothing else
> had worked, such as with his poor sister. None of this had the least bear-
> ing on his situation. The love that would overcome him was of a differ-
> ent order entirely. It was not the kind that could be used for the child's
> improvement or his own. It was love without reason, love for something
> futureless, love that appeared to exist only to be itself, imperious and all
> demanding, the kind that would cause him to make a fool of himself in
> an instant. And it only began with Bishop. It began with Bishop and then
> like an avalanche covered everything his reason hated. He always felt
> with it a rush of longing to have the old man's eyes—insane, fish-colored,
> violent with their impossible vision of a world transfigured—turned on
> him once again. The longing was like an undertow in his blood dragging
> him backwards to what he knew to be madness. (*TVBIA*, 192)

Rayber cannot abide the mystery of his inexplicable love for Bishop. As
Old Tarwater says of him, "He don't know it's anything he can't know"
(*TVBIA*, 156).

The consequence of Rayber's willful and stubborn asceticism, of his
denial of "love without reason," was an indifference to life—even his own.
Lying in bed at the Cherokee Lodge, knowing that Tarwater had taken
Bishop out in the rowboat to drown him, Rayber thought to himself that

> all he would be was an observer. He waited with serenity. Life had never
> been good enough to him for him to wince at its destruction. He told
> himself that he was indifferent even to his own dissolution. It seemed to
> him that this indifference was the most that human dignity could
> achieve, and for the moment forgetting his lapses, forgetting even his
> narrow escape of the afternoon, he felt he had achieved it. To feel noth-
> ing was peace. (*TVBIA*, 241)

Nevertheless, Rayber awaits the pain of Bishop's loss in order to demonstrate the strength of his denial of love and his embrace of the most that
"human dignity could achieve," but he is denied his pain. His indifference bears the fruit of its barrenness.

> He stared out over the empty still pond to the dark wood that sur-
> rounded it. The boy would be moving off through it to meet his
> appalling destiny. He knew with an instinct as sure as the dull mechanical

beat of his heart that he had baptized the child even as he drowned him, that he was headed for everything the old man had prepared him for, that he moved off now through the black forest toward a violent encounter with his fate. (*TVBIA*, 242–43)

He stood waiting for the raging pain, the intolerable hurt that was his due, to begin, so that he could ignore it, but he continued to feel nothing. He stood light-headed at the window and it was not until he realized there would be no pain that he collapsed. (*TVBIA*, 243)

Rayber's strength of denial, his iron-clad will to embrace nothing, defines his role in the story; but when O'Connor permits him to collapse after realizing there will be no raging pain to deny, the reader recognizes that there may be hope that Rayber will accept the divine love he fears.

The divine presence reveals It-self to Tarwater as a silence that manifests itself in the visible-material cosmos to include Tarwater's embodied consciousness. This silence appears to Tarwater in the landscape; in his Tarwater blood and the blood of the prophets; in his hunger; and, sometimes, in the stars above.[37] In addition to the silence as it appears in the landscape, the silence "speaks" in the blood of Tarwater: as he receives the divine command in his final vision, "The words were as silent as seeds opening one at a time in his blood" (*TVBIA*, 267). Or the silence may infuse the hunger that he experienced and could not satisfy with food after leaving Powderhead: "Since the breakfast he had finished sitting in the presence of his uncle's corpse, he had not been satisfied by food, and his hunger had become like an insistent silent

37. There are twenty-five passages in *The Violent Bear It Away* where *silence* or some variant appears with reference to Tarwater. I cannot comment on all these passages, but I list the phrases or clauses here: "the silent woods that encircled them" (159); "the old man's words had been dropping one by one into him and now, silent, hidden in his bloodstream" (159); "alone in the presence of an immense silent eye" (174); "The quiet seemed palpable" (174); "the implacable silence descended around him" (174); "the revelation came, silent, implacable" (178); "sound was saturated in silence" (178); "his silent adversary" (179); "a continual struggle with the silence that confronted him" (218); "a strange waiting silence" (218); "the silent country" (218); "the silence was about to surround him" (218); "an insistent silent force inside him" (219); "a silence inside akin to the silence outside" (219); "threatening the silence" (220); "hush in his blood and a stillness in the atmosphere" (220); "distinct tension in the quiet" (221); "friend was silent" (221); "flinging the silent words at the silent face" (221); "the light silent eyes of the child " (251); "the country which seemed to lie beyond the silence" (255); "two silent serene eyes were gazing at him" (256); "A deep-filled quiet pervaded everything" (265); "words were as silent as seeds" (266); "that violent country where the silence is never broken" (267).

force inside him, a silence inside akin to the silence outside, as if the grand trap left him barely an inch to move in, barely an inch in which to keep himself inviolate" (*TVBIA*, 219). The stars also participate in the silent manifestation of the divine presence. Sitting on the doorstep of his uncle's house in the city, "he was unpleasantly aware of the stars. They seemed to be holes in his skull through which some distant unmoving light was watching him. It was as if he were alone in the presence of an immense silent eye" (*TVBIA*, 174). Every time the silence almost persuades Tarwater to baptize Bishop, thereby accepting his vocation, the devil in the form of the stranger-friend who speaks in Tarwater's voice advises him to ignore such "sensations," for his call must be as dramatic as God's dealings with the Old Testament prophets.

> Tarwater could have baptized him any one of a hundred times without so much as touching him. Each time the temptation came, he would feel that the silence was about to surround him and he was going to be lost in it forever. He would have fallen but for the wise voice that sustained him—the stranger who had kept him company while he dug his uncle's grave.
>
> Sensations, his friend—no longer a stranger—said. Feelings. What you want is a sign, a real sign, suitable to a prophet. If you are a prophet, it's only right you should be treated like one. When Jonah dallied, he was cast three days in a belly of darkness and vomited up in the place of his mission. That was a sign; it wasn't no sensation. (*TVBIA*, 218–19)

There are two particularly powerful instances of the divine presence manifesting itself in silence to Tarwater that stand out: the moment when the revelation came to him that he was called to baptize Bishop and to prophesy, and the moment when he finally accepted the divine call of his prophecy. The first instance occurs right after Tarwater has hitched a ride to Rayber's house. We have already seen Tarwater waiting on Rayber's stoop and sensing that the stars above were holes in his head through which an "immense silent eye" watched. After Rayber opens the door and Tarwater has entered, he sees Bishop in the hallway peering at him, "dim and ancient, like a child who had been a child for centuries" (*TVBIA*, 177).

> Tarwater clenched his fists. He stood like one condemned, waiting at the spot of execution. Then the revelation came, silent, implacable, direct as a bullet. He did not look into the eyes of any fiery beast or see a burning bush. He only knew, with a certainty sunk in despair, that he was

expected to baptize the child he saw and begin the life his great-uncle had prepared him for. He knew that he was called to be a prophet and that the ways of his prophecy would not be remarkable. His black pupils, glassy and still, reflected depth on depth his own stricken image of himself, trudging into the distance in the bleeding stinking mad shadow of Jesus, until at last he received his reward, a broken fish, a multiplied loaf. The Lord out of dust had created him, had made him blood and nerve and mind, had made him to bleed and weep and think, and set him in a world of loss and fire all to baptize one idiot child that He need not have created in the first place and to cry out a gospel just as foolish. He tried to shout, "NO!" but it was like trying to shout in his sleep. The sound was saturated in silence, lost. (*TVBIA*, 177–78)

After Tarwater has drowned-baptized Bishop, he feels assured that he has successfully defied God's plan for his life. As he trudges home to Powderhead, which he now believes his own to do with as he wishes, he thinks that his act has saved him from the fate of "trudging off into the distance in the bleeding stinking mad shadow of Jesus, lost forever to his own inclinations." (*TVBIA*, 254–55). But that he spoke the words of baptism as he drowned Bishop disturbs him. He reasons with himself: "It was an accident and nothing more. He considered only that the boy was drowned and that he had done it, and that in the order of things, a drowning was a more important act than a few words spilled in the water" (*TVBIA*, 255). He was once again, however, aware "of the country which seemed to lie beyond the silence, or in it, stretching off into the distance around him" (*TVBIA*, 255).

But then Tarwater is raped by the stranger who drives a "lavender and cream-colored car," and by this act of violation, he is prepared to receive his moment of grace, as Old Tarwater had prepared him. Arriving at Powderhead, he is sent the vision of Old Tarwater finding his place on the hillside to be fed by the loaves and fishes, the "bread of life" that he hungered for, a vision Tarwater now recognizes as the source of his own hunger. Tarwater is granted a second vision, a second call, to which he can now respond with acceptance.

There, rising and spreading in the night, a red-gold tree of fire ascended as if it would consume the darkness in one tremendous burst of flame. The boy's breath went out to meet it. He knew that this was the fire that had encircled Daniel, that had raised Elijah from the earth, that had spoken to Moses and would in the instant speak to him. He threw himself to the ground and with his face against the dirt of the grave, he heard the command. GO WARN THE CHILDREN OF GOD OF THE TERRIBLE SPEED OF MERCY. The words were as silent as seeds opening one at a time in his blood. (*TVBIA,* 267)

Now lost to his old intentions, "he moved steadily on, his face set toward the dark city, where the children of God lay sleeping" (*TVBIA,* 267).

EPILOGUE

## "Our Love of Life, Children, Our Love of Life"

He begins to leave who begins to love.
Many the leaving who know it not,
for the feet of those leaving are affections of the heart:
and yet, they are leaving Babylon.

~ SAINT AUGUSTINE, *ENARRATIONES IN PSALMOS*

St. Cyril of Jerusalem, in instructing catechumens, wrote: "The dragon sits by the side of the road, watching those who pass. Beware lest he devour you. We go to the Father of Souls, but it is necessary to pass by the dragon." No matter what form the dragon may take, it is of this mysterious passage past him, or into his jaws, that stories of any depth will always be concerned to tell, and this being the case, it requires considerable courage at any time, in any country, not to turn away from the storyteller.

~ FLANNERY O'CONNOR, "THE FICTION WRITER AND HIS COUNTRY"

---

"I dropped to depth,/And then I leaped to height," writes poet Richard Eberhart, "But in between was the fearsome place."[1] In the fearsome place—between the Timeless depth of our Beginning and the height of Beyond as it Timelessly orders our existence—the Time of the Tale symbolizes the human struggle to dwell in

1. Richard Eberhart, "Birth and Death," in *Collected Poems, 1930–1986*, 226.

141

the presence of the present and to live in conscious awareness of our mortal-immortal nature. In writing of the Time of the Tale, Voegelin expressed his meditative insight into the nexus between timeless Being and being-in-time, putting a name to the literary symbolization of that commingling. The Time of the Tale, he wrote, "expresses the experience of being (that embraces all sorts of reality, the cosmos) in flux." The cosmos with "all sorts of reality" encompasses "being-things," all things that exist in time and have their existence because they are embraced by and participate in the Timeless Being of the It-reality. The mystery of reality, however, reveals by a reason unfathomable to us that all things emerge into time from the Timeless depth and disappear back into that nonexistent, timeless Apeiron. "To exist," says Voegelin, following Anaximander, "means to participate in two modes of reality: (1) in the Apeiron as the timeless *arche* of things and (2) in the ordered succession of things as the manifestation of the Apeiron in time."[2] In human consciousness we experience this process of existing in time while immersed in a timeless reality as an "In-Between reality, governed by the tension of life and death."[3] In the In-Between reality of the *metaxy,* "time," as Plato observed, is the "*eikon* of eternity." The thing-reality of the body is embraced by Being, the nonexistent It-reality; that is, Being is present in and orders *all* being-things of the cosmos. We say also that all being-things participate in Being. In human consciousness, we become aware of our In-Between status as we struggle to live our lives under the judgment of death.

The linguistic expressions of our struggles to order our thing-bound, time-bound lives in the light of our participation in the Timeless Beyond are symbolized in the Time of the Tale and will always recall the form of myth, which seeks to combine cosmic, human, and divine elements. Specific Tales vary depending upon whether the experiential accent falls on the Beginning, the *metaxy,* or the Beyond; but the Tale, to be authentic, must always comprehend both the temporal and the timeless elements of reality as they reveal themselves in the cosmic, human, and divine realms. The following chart illustrates this spectrum in the Tales with examples.

2. Voegelin, *Ecumenic Age,* 233.
3. Ibid.

BEGINNING:
    Content:   The Timeless creates the cosmos and thus time
    Form:       Myth that combines cosmic, human, and divine elements
        EXAMPLES: Creation stories of various cultures.
                   Genesis I

*METAXY:*
    Content:   The Timeless in time
    Form:       Myth that combines cosmic, human, and divine elements
        EXAMPLES: The Gospels
                   *The Violent Bear It Away*

BEYOND:
    Content:   The Timeless beyond time
    Form:       Myth that combines cosmic, human, and divine elements
        EXAMPLES: Plato's Saving Tale
                   Saint Paul's Apocalypse
                   Tarwater's vision of the "bread of life" in *The Violent*
                   *Bear It Away*

These Tales—whether they accent the Beginning or the Beyond—collapse into the Time of the Tale as it is told in the *metaxy,* for the In-Between is the only spatio-metaphorical-ontological locus where the writer can symbolize, imaginatively and linguistically, participation in the cosmic, human, and divine elements of reality through the body, intellect, imagination, soul, and spirit of his composite nature. The *metaxy,* in addition to being the "place" in which humans recognize the primary experience of the cosmos, in which they know themselves as mortal-immortal beings, assumes via the Time of the Tale the literary function of recovering a foundational wholeness that nonetheless encompasses the differentiations that distinguish the now-immanent cosmos from the Transcendent Timeless. In other words, the Time of the Tale now assumes the function of the *metaxy,* the In-Between of Beginning and Beyond that expresses the wholeness of reality.

Even though the cosmos had, in noetic and pneumatic differentiations, become the immanent world demarcated from the divine ground of Being, the primary experience never disappears. As Voegelin observed, even Immanuel Kant had to admit:

"Two things fill the mind with ever new and increasing admiration and awe: the starry heaven above me and the moral law within me." Kant's "starry heaven" is the celestial universe transparent for its divine ground, and his "moral law" is the presence of a divine reality that has become transmundane in the conscious existence of a man who has become mundane. The In-Between reality of the primary experience has been critically pruned; it is no longer the model for symbolizing all modes of reality; but it is still there.[4]

Developments in modern natural science, generally understood as focused upon the exploration of the immanent world of material thing-reality, have brought back into focus the primary experience of the cosmos latent in the scientific worldview. Relying upon discoveries made in the twentieth-century by physicist Albert Einstein and mathematician Hermann Minkowski, Voegelin recognized, in his speculations about simultaneity, that the wholeness of the primary experience of the cosmos is achieved through the medium of sense perception as light with its high velocity makes present the cosmos to the human eye. In "The Moving Soul," he writes:

> In order to have the kind of "sense perception" with which we are familiar, light must move with a velocity sufficiently large to give it practical simultaneity at all points of man's pragmatic range. Only with light moving at a high velocity can we have the instantaneous experience of reality that we have.

> That the reality surrounding us is the intelligible whole of a cosmos cannot be derived from the experience of physical reality. Rather, the conception of the intelligible whole articulates the impact of the cosmos on the eye, as in the Xenophantic exclamation, reported by Aristotle, "Looking up at the expanse of the Heaven 'The One, he said, is the God.'" And because the One of spontaneous presence is the God, the cosmic One must partake of divine eternity.

The "experience of physical reality" (perception, constructs, memory) is bound to the primary experience of the cosmos in the "look at the Heaven."[5]

4. Ibid., 128.
5. Voegelin, "The Moving Soul," 170, 172.

It is the Time of the Tale, however, that linguistically restores the wholeness of the primary experience necessary to human beings who ask why? and wherefore? The Tale is essential to human life, for only in the Time of the Tale is Being in flux symbolized. For this reason, it is important that philosophy, in its quest to recover reality, take notice of literature in its various forms.

Flannery O'Connor asserts that "it takes considerable courage at any time . . . not to turn away from the storyteller," because the storyteller reminds us that we must pass by the dragon to reach the Father of Souls. The mysterious passage is the fearsome place of the In-Between, where we struggle in time to experience love and meaning that are lasting and timeless. When, invoking our freedom to respond to or deny the divine appeal, we refuse the mysterious journey to the Father of Souls, we deform our own wholeness as composite beings of the In-Between. Stories "of any depth," O'Connor implies, confront the wholeness of human nature and the enfolding reality.

Not all stories will rise to the level of the Time of the Tale. Sometimes an author will symbolize deformation that obscures, even while revealing, the wholeness of reality and human experience. I wish now to recall four characters from the novels and their experiences of the fearsome place: Tom Crick, narrator of *Waterland;* Georg von Geyrenhoff, "narrator" of *The Demons;* and Francis Marion Tarwater and his uncle, Rayber, of *The Violent Bear It Away.* Tom Crick and Geyrenhoff chose for themselves the role of observer, while Tarwater and Rayber are fiercely engaged in the In-Between of their fearsome place. Eventually, it is true, both Tom Crick and Geyrenhoff become participants in life, but their participation issues in different results. Tom, as a child, had always been an observer,

> until a series of encounters with the Here and Now gave a sudden pointedness to my studies. Until the Here and Now, gripping me by the arm, slapping my face and telling me to take a good look at the mess I was in, informed me that history was no invention but indeed existed—and I had become part of it. (*W,* 62)

But he becomes fully cognizant of the impact of his actions upon his own life as well as the lives of his friends and family. When his brother Dick kills Freddie, when he and Mary abort their baby, and when Dick dives into the Ouse to swim to the sea, Tom embarks on a lifetime of professional observation by becoming a historian and a teacher of history. His research into his own life was motivated by his desire to discover when things began to go wrong and why, because certainly when Dick killed Freddie, when Mary and Tom killed their baby, and when Dick plunged into the Ouse, things had gone wrong. Presumably his historical education confirmed for him the view that the divine was not an element in the reality that he scoured for understanding and meaning. "What history teaches us," says Tom, "is to avoid illusion and make-believe, to lay aside dreams, moonshine, cure-alls, wonder-workings, pie-in-the-sky—to be realistic" (*W*, 108). His conception of history only confirmed for him what his father, Henry Crick, had told him when he was ten years old: "'Do you know what the stars are? They are the silver dust of God's blessing. They are little broken-off bits of heaven. God cast them down to fall on us. But when he saw how wicked we were, he changed his mind and ordered the stars to stop" (*W*, 1–2).

Tom Crick's historical search, his *historia*, his inquiry into the past to discover why things went wrong, led him to conclude that Natural History was always "getting the better of" Artificial History—full of "revolutionaries, prophets of new worlds, and even humble champions of Progress" building and reforming empires. And Natural History is that "unfathomable stuff we're made from . . . our love of life, children, our love of life" that we keep coming back to (*W*, 205). Tom furthermore urges his students always to be curious, for curiosity "begets love. It weds us to the world. It's part of our perverse, madcap love for this impossible planet we inhabit" (*W*, 206). Tom is correct. Curiosity begets love, and love weds us to the world and leads us on to the love of life that cannot be repressed, for it is always bursting forth in the midst of the world-making actions of the "champions of Progress."

Something, however, is amiss in *Waterland*. Even though all of the components of the Time of the Tale—the cosmic, human, and divine—are present (the divine, however, is only for children and "simple, backward people in God-forsaken places"), Tom's spiritual education, exemplified in his father's story about stars, prevents him from understanding and embracing the mortal-immortal In-Between of the primary experience. Tom does experience the fearsome place, but it is the fearsome place of human mortality where stories have to be made up and told to calm our fears. Human beings have become simply natural beings in Tom's world. Despite all of his apparently correct assertions about human nature—"But man—let me offer you a definition—is the story-telling animal" (*W*, 62); "Another definition of Man: the animal which demands an explanation, the animal which asks Why" (*W*,

106); "Another definition of Man: the animal who craves meaning—but knows—" (*W*, 140)—somehow Tom misses the point about human beings and human history. Yes, human beings ask why, demand explanation, crave meaning, but some, like Tom, "know" history is only "a lucky dip of meanings" and that "events elude meaning." Tom's "love of life, children, love of life" sounds the right knell; but if this "love of life" is simply an animal cry for survival and if human beings only tell stories to assuage their fears, what is it that we love in this life? Tom's genuine love—of Mary, of his students—weds him to the world. When he says to his students that our curiosity is "part of our perverse, madcap love for his impossible planet we inhabit," he is speaking of his own love of life. However, despite all of his overt recognition that humans ask why and search for explanations and demand meaning, Tom fails to see that the real Why questions—those of Leibniz, for example—would demand that he explore not only the natural history of the eel but also the natural history of man's search for meaning; would demand that he recognize that the first question "why" leads to the ultimate question, Why.

Perhaps I am too harsh on Tom; but if we look at the end of his story, what do we see? Tom's search did not yield the beginning he sought, and in the end it only filled his years with stories that yielded no comfort. In the story line of the present, 1980, Mary has been locked up in a mental institution because she stole a baby under the illusion that God had commanded it, and Tom has been forced into retirement and will soon be deprived of "his children," his students. Tom ends the book not in 1980, but in 1943, with the death of Dick Crick, "a fish of a man," his half-brother sired by his mother's father. He cannot make meaning out of the story, for neither he nor Mary could find forgiveness for their actions—the consequences of a curiosity that once bound them to the world through the begetting of love. His search only looks like a "precious bag of clues" saved from the summer of 1943, which becomes a source of stories to tell his "children" to assuage their fears, and his, of the end of the world.

The story that Tom tells is not without some glimmer of hope—perhaps not for Tom but for those readers who have the courage "not to turn away from the storyteller." Tom's definitions of human nature carry within them hope; for in the full consciousness of participation in all the realms of Being we cannot fail to see that when we ask the first question "when did things go wrong," we will finally come to the ultimate question of Why. And even though Tom moves further and further back into time to reach the beginning of when things began to go wrong, so far back that he comes to the cosmic time of the mysterious and ongoing origins of the eel, the reader can recognize with Aristotle that an infinite regress of beginnings leads nowhere. Tom's Tale can lead us into our own loving search for the truth of our existence if we accept Tom's unwitting demonstration that a search conducted by an animal that asks why is itself a recognition that the man who asks why is more than an animal.

Department Councillor Geyrenhoff, "narrator" of *The Demons*, tells a different story. His is the story of a pensioner who decides to observe and chronicle the life of *die Unsrigen*, composed of a cross-section of Viennese society. In order to chronicle the actions of such a group, Geyrenhoff resolved to be objective, which meant for him that he would be indifferent to the various activities of the members. Because of the second reality from which his indifference arises and in which he had been living since his fourteenth year, Geyrenhoff was unable to understand what was happening in the life that was going on right under his nose. As the result of a series of events connected with certain members of the *die Unsrigen*, events that led him into the life of the widow Friederike Ruthmayr as well as events that led him to question his own integrity and apperception, Geyrenhoff begins to emerge from his life in second reality. As he begins to emerge from second reality, Geyrenhoff, in reflecting back upon the past years and months, realizes that his objectivity and supposed detachment from the goings-on of *die Unsrigen* had resulted in his becoming indifferent to life itself. He remembers:

> Indifference gripped me, but this grip was not gentle, not reassuring; it was icy, hinted at fearful terrors. I realized at once that indifference does not permit an objective view of things, as might at first appear. It blocks one's view. Indifference blinds. Nor does it remain indifference; it degenerates rapidly into disgust with life. (*D*, 845)

When the reality that is external to him begins to penetrate his indifference, Geyrenhoff is put on a trajectory that leads him to love Friederike Ruthmayr. His complete and conscious reentry into full participation in life, however, comes only when he sees Imre Gyurkicz killed and can say with conviction, "He was a friend of mine." Intoning the "De Profundis" with his mentor, Hofrat Gürtzner-Gontard, Geyrenhoff recognizes *die Tiefe ist aussen* and embraces his full humanity.

The courage that O'Connor's Rayber exhibits in turning away from the biblical tradition of his upbringing is a false courage that results in an indifference to life, including his own. The real courage comes only as we turn *to* the storyteller and stories of the depth that reveal to us the pureness and clarity of a love that confirms not only the mortality of our shared humanity but also the immortality of the ground of Being from which we emerge, in which we participate, and in which we are enfolded.

Tarwater's love of life is mediated through his acceptance and love of God. Only when he accepts God's vocation and mission for him is he able to engage his vocation of prophecy without the dread of "trudging into the distance in the bleeding stinking mad shadow of Jesus." He cannot bring to the children of God the bread of life until he comprehends in his prophet's blood that his bodily hunger was the spiritual hunger that could only be fed by responding to the Beyond.

> He felt his hunger no longer as a pain but as a tide. He felt it rising in himself through time and darkness, rising through the centuries, and he knew that it rose in a line of men whose lives were chosen to sustain it, who would wander in the world, strangers from that violent country where the silence is never broken except to shout the truth. He felt it building from the blood of Abel to his own, rising and engulfing him. (*TVBIA*, 266–67)

The great Russian novelist Fyodor Dostoyevsky reminds us too that love of life and love of the world must be rooted in love of the divine ground. If it is not, then "all is permitted," and man embraces the fear and terror of nothingness and the hatred of all creation, including himself. In *The Brothers Karamazov*, Dostoyevsky gave the expression of this belief to Father Zossima, who said:

> "Much on earth is hidden from us, but to make up for that we have been given a precious mystic sense of our living bond with the other world, with the higher heavenly world, and the roots of our thoughts and feelings are not here but in other worlds. . . .
> "God took seeds from different worlds and sowed them on this earth, and His garden grew up and everything came up that could come up. But what grows lives and is alive only through the feeling of its contact with other mysterious worlds. If that feeling grows weak or is destroyed in you, the heavenly growth will die away in you. Then you will be indifferent to life and even grow to hate it. That's what I think."[6]

---

6. Dostoyevsky, *The Brothers Karamazov*, 296.

"A novel is an exceedingly ordinary thing: it wades through lived experience," wrote Péter Nádas.[7] And we agree, the novel certainly *does* wade through "*lived* experience." But is the novel an "exceedingly *ordinary* thing"? Ordinary only if we mean that it arises from an individual's experience of the fearsome place of the In-Between and speaks to everyone's need to understand why we must die while yet we want to live. In his essay "Humane Literacy," George Steiner writes, "All great writing springs from *le dur désir de durer,* the harsh contrivance of spirit against death, the hope to overreach time by force of creation."[8] All great reading also "springs from *le dur désir de durer,*" and in a great novel, we readers participate with the writer in the "harsh contrivance of spirit against death." Art does not save us, but in our time art preserves for us a space in which we can be reminded of the story that is told by human beings in search of their humanity and the truth of their existence. It reminds us that the search is crucial to the love of life and that love of life is crucial to our search for the truth of our existence.

7. Nádas, "Novelist and His Selfs," 18.
8. Steiner, "Humane Literacy," 3.

# Brief Overview of Literary Topics

*Robert B. Heilman and Eric Voegelin:*
*A Friendship in Letters, 1944–1984*

The correspondence contains 151 letters;[1] 78 were written by Heilman and 73 by Voegelin. While the correspondence records a lifelong friendship, literary topics account for a large portion of the total volume. Of the 78 letters that Heilman wrote, 62 contain at least one literary reference, ranging from relatively minor inquiries after Voegelin's work to discourses on literary topics; of the 73 letters Voegelin wrote, 48 contain such references.

In his letters to Heilman, Voegelin mentions thirty-two literary figures of the modern era including writers such as Hermann Broch, Heimito von Doderer, Dostoyevsky, Eliot, Flaubert, Joyce, Miguel Unamuno, and Paul Valéry. While eighteen of these receive a brief mention in only one letter, eleven of the thirty-two are accompanied by substantive comments. Thomas Mann falls into this group; Voegelin writes in letter 22:

> I just finished reading Thomas Mann's *Doctor Faustus.* With mixed feelings. It will interest you as a further experiment in writing a novel, without a society of which one could write an epic, using mystical symbols as the instrument for interpreting the German catastrophe. While the thing as a whole is an awe-inspiring performance, I am not quite happy about this simplification of the German problem into a daemonic

---

1. An additional letter from Lissy Voegelin to Heilman granting him permission to dedicate his book *Magic in the Web: Action and Language in Othello* to Eric and thanking him for honoring her husband, is included in the book. Consequently, the book contains a total of 152 letters.

Germany whose story is written [by] the humanistic German Mann. The
weakness of Mann begins to show more than in earlier works. There is,
for instance, a conversation between the hero and the devil; it invites
comparison between the similar conversations in the *Karamazovs* and in
Unamuno's *Nivola*—and the comparison is not too good for Mann. (77)

Others, such as D. H. Lawrence (*AFIL,* letter 91, January 14, 1961, pp.
209–11) and Gustave Flaubert (*AFIL,* letter 107, February 22, 1965, p.
233), appear in this group of eleven mentioned in only one letter.

Nine ancient or medieval writers are mentioned and include
Aeschylus, Aristotle, Dante, Euripides, Heraclitus, Herodotus, Hesiod,
Homer, and Plato. One of Voegelin's more interesting comments on
Homer comes in July 1951 while Voegelin is in the midst of writing and
revising his work on Homer for the planned *History of Political Ideas.*
He writes:

> I am teaching summer-school this year because the revision work that I
> am doing now can be done best at home. Still, some new items have to
> be added. Just now it is the turn of Homer who hitherto did not have a
> chapter because I had not developed the methods for analyzing the very
> complicated psychology in which divine inspirations, predictions of fate,
> dreams, conferences among the gods, etc., function as the unconscious.
> But now I can do it—or at least I fondly believe I can. The wrath of
> Achilles is already dissected to its last corner; and the fascination of
> Helena (a juicy morsel) is practically cleared up. In the course of this
> work I have become a firm believer in the existence of Homer; somebody
> *must* have written these intricately constructed works; they cannot have
> grown like Topsy as German philologists still maintain. (*AFIL,* letter 31,
> July 7, 1951, p. 93)

As could be expected in a correspondence with a Shakespeare
scholar, Shakespeare appears in many of Voegelin's letters. Finally,
Henry James benefits from an extensive commentary in an early letter
on *The Turn of the Screw* (letter 11, November 13, 1947), with brief
mentions during the period that Voegelin was writing a postscript to
the letter that would be published in the *Southern Review.*

From a different perspective, various clusters of letters that contain
significant and extensive commentary on literary topics or commentary
growing from literary stimuli emerge during the course of the correspondence. There is one major exchange of letters (letters 63–66) where
Voegelin, in letters 63 and 65, substantively responds to Heilman's

dedication of his book *Magic in the Web: Action and Language in Othello* to him. In these two letters Voegelin articulates many of the principles upon which he relies when he interprets literature. I focus on these letters in chapter 1. Four exchanges of letters contain significant statements by Voegelin on literature; in most of these exchanges, Voegelin articulates his ideas as responses to various stimuli provided by Heilman in one of his letters. These four exchanges include:

Letters 35–**36**[2] (1952), occasioned by Heilman's proposal of a "higher" or "transcendental pragmatism." Voegelin's letter includes references to Aristotle's *bios theoretikos,* Hebrews 11:1, "things unseen of Solonic and Heraclitean origin," and the Thomistic *analogia entis.*

Letters **37**–38–**39** (1952), occasioned by Heilman's close, editorial reading of a manuscript that four years later would be published as "Introduction: The Symbolization of Order," to *Order and History* as well as to volume I, *Israel and Revelation.* Voegelin refers to Descartes's *Cogito ergo sum,* Baader's *Cogitor ergo sum,* and to the conflict between literary convention and philosophical language.

Letters 83–**84**–85 (1959), occasioned by Heilman's publication "Fashions in Melodrama." Voegelin addresses Heilman's statement that "war is all melodrama; so is politics." He mentions Carl Schmitt, *philia politike,* the psychology of passion, the Hobbesian fallacy that the life of passion is the essence of man, passion and spirit, and his visit to the Cimétière Marin of Paul Valéry.

Letters 106–**107**–108 (1965), occasioned by Heilman's discussion of his work on *Tragedy and Melodrama* and his comments on "expressionistic morality." Voegelin includes references to Orwell, Dostoyevsky, Doderer, Max Frisch, Friedrich Dürrenmatt, the *burlesque* and the *grotesque,* Flaubert, Sartre, and Brecht.

There are three minor exchanges that either deal with specifically narrow topics arising out of a publication or that do not seem to be contributing to a conversation on complementary themes being developed in each man's research:

---

2. Voegelin letter numbers appear in boldface type.

Letters **48**–49 (1954) focused on a specific reaction to the manner of Voegelin's portrayal of Homer's characters in Voegelin's publication "The World of Homer."

Letters **103**–104 (1964) were occasioned by Voegelin's report to Heilman on his lecture "Versuch zu einer Philosophie der Geschichte" to the Institut für Politische Wissenschaften in Salzburg, Austria.[3] Persons mentioned include Proust and Shakespeare (*Richard II*).

Letters 122–**123** (1969) focused on issues arising from Voegelin's "Postscript: On Paradise and Revolution" for publication in the *Southern Review*. This exchange resulted in Voegelin's interesting exposition on the origins of the phenomenon of understatement in English philosophy and thought. Persons mentioned include Hobbes, Locke, Berkeley, Hume, Thomas Reid, John Dewey, and Edmund Burke.

Finally, in several letters Voegelin makes significant remarks about literature that do not elicit a written response from Heilman:

Letter **9** (1946). Voegelin comments on Heilman's *King Lear* manuscript and includes six quotations, apparently translated by Voegelin, from Goethe's *Shakespeare und kein Ende* (1813).

Letter **11** (1947). Voegelin comments on Henry James's *The Turn of the Screw*.

Letter **91** (1961). Voegelin comments extensively on D. H. Lawrence and related issues after reading a review by Heilman of Eliseo Vivas, *D. H. Lawrence: The Failure and the Triumph of Art*. Other persons mentioned include Hölderlin (Odes), Frank Wedekind (*Frühlingserwachen, Lulu,* or *Minnehaha*), Spengler (*Decline of the West*), Alfred Kinsey, and Aristotle (*Poetics*).

Letter **110** (1966). Voegelin reports to Heilman on the development of his work as it appeared in the German publication of *Anamnesis*.

---

3. Discussion notes and correspondence relating to this speech may be found in Eric Voegelin Papers, Hoover Institution Archives, box 72, file 4.

APPENDIX 2

*Waterland*

Primary Characters and Setting

**Tom Crick** (1927– ): comprehensive school history teacher, historian, narrator of the story, son of **Henry Crick** (1899–1947; died of bronco-pneumonia, i.e. phlegm) and **Helen** Crick née Atkinson (1896–1937; died of the East Wind flu).

**Mary Crick** (1927– ): née Metcalf, wife of Tom Crick.

**Dick Crick** (1923–1943): Tom's "potato-head" half-brother and son of **Ernest Richard Atkinson** (1874–1922) and his daughter Helen Crick née Atkinson (1896–1937), dredger on the *Rosa II* and killer of Freddie Parr.

**Freddie Parr** (c. 1927–1943): adolescent friend of Tom, Dick, and Mary.

**Price:** Tom's prized history student in whom he sees the melancholy and concern for the future of his own grandfather, Ernest Richard Atkinson, and whom he claims, while drinking in a club with Price, as his son.

**The Atkinsons:** Tom's ancestors on his mother's side, brewers, partisans of the Idea of Progress, and captains of commerce.

**Ernest Richard Atkinson** (1874–1922): A melancholy and moody man, who "wished for nothing more than to be an honest and unambitious purveyor of barrels of happiness." Presided over the decline of the Atkinson commercial empire. Dick's father and grandfather and Tom's grandfather. Committed suicide on September 26, 1922.

**The Cricks:** Tom's ancestors on his father's side, water people, lock-keepers, dredgers, and storytellers.

**Setting:** the Fens of eastern England. A flat, lowland "network of swamps and brackish lagoons," 1,200 square miles in area "bounded to the east by the limestone hills of the Midlands, to the south and east by the chalk hills of Cambridgeshire, Suffolk and Norfolk," and drained to the north by the Great Ouse river that empties into the North Sea at the Wash.

**Time(s):** of present narration, 1980.
of remembered-recounted events, 1940s.
of various historical researches, 4th c. BC to 1937.

APPENDIX 3

*Waterland*

Chronology by Chapter Title[1]

1 About the Stars and the Sluice (1937)
2 About the End of History (1980)
3 About the Fens (c. 697–1922)
4 Before the Headmaster (1980)
5 A Bruise upon a Bruise (1943)
6 An Empty Vessel (1979; 1943–1947)
7 About Holes and Things (1942–1943)
8 About the Story-telling Animal (1980)
9 About the Rise of the Atkinsons (1751–1874)
10 About the Question Why (1980)
11 About Accidental Death (1943)
12 About the Change of Life (1943–1980)
13 Histrionics (1943)
14 De la Révolution (1980)
15 About the Ouse (to 1800s)
16 Longitude 0° (1980)
17 About the Lock Keeper (1918–1943)
18 In Loco Parentis (1980)
19 About my Grandfather (1874–1910)
20 The Explanation of Explanation (1980)
21 Aux Armes (1980)
22 About Coronation Ale (1910–1914)

1. The story is told in 1980 as a series of flashbacks and disquisitions on various subjects. The dates assigned to chapters indicate the time (or times in some cases) of the events recounted in the chapter. Note also that I have supplied chapter numbers for convenience, even though chapter numbers do not appear in the book as published.

23 Quatorze Juillet (1980)
24 Child's Play (1940)
25 Forget the Bastille (1980)
26 About the Eel (ancient times to 1920s)
27 About Natural History (1980)
28 And Artificial History (1940)
29 Detective Work (1943)
30 About the Saviour of the World (1914–1922)
31 A Teacher's Testament (1980)
32 About Beauty and the Beast (1937–1943)
33 Who Says? (1980)
34 Too Big (1943)
35 Unknown Country (1980)
36 About Nothing (1980)
37 Le Jour de Gras (1980)
38 About the East Wind (1937)
39 Stupid (1943)
40 About Contemporary Nightmares (1980)
41 A Feeling in the Guts (1980; 1943)
42 About the Witch (1943)
43 Not So Final (1980)
44 Begin Again (1980)
45 About the Pike (1943)
46 About my Grandfather's Chest (1943)
47 Goodnight (1980)
48 And Adieu (1980)
49 About Empire Building (1980)
50 The Whole Story (1947)
51 About Phlegm (1980)
52 About the Rosa II (1943)

# APPENDIX 4

## Characters from *The Demons* Included in Chapter 5

Although there are 142 characters in the novel, 31 of whom are designated as principal by the translators, I have limited my analysis to the following.

**Alois Gach.** Gach is a former sergeant of Captain Ruthmayr's regiment. He was given the responsibility of delivering his captain's will, which established an inheritance for Charlotte von Schlaggenberg, to Financial Counsellor Levielle.

**Georg von Geyrenhoff.** A retired civil servant, Geyrenhoff is the narrator and proposes to chronicle the story of what he calls *die Unsrigen* ("Our Crowd"). He lives in Döbling, a suburb of Vienna, in a studio that looks out over the city, and is financially independent, having retired early from the civil service and having just received the bounty of released resources that had been held in England after World War I. Geyrenhoff soon discovers that he is not a good chronicler because he misunderstands several key characters and misinterprets information. His intention to write the chronicle is completely derailed and he gives it up (only to jot down a few notes) when he becomes involved (at first accidentally) in the uncovering of the plot to disinherit Charlotte von Schlaggenberg (Quapp). As chronicler of the story, Geyrenhoff is replaced by an omniscient narrator.

**Hofrat von Gürtzner-Gontard.** Geyrenhoff's former superior (in the civil service) for whom Geyrenhoff possesses great respect and who provides Geyrenhoff crucial information on the relationship between second reality and revolution.

**Mary K.** A widow who lost a leg in a streetcar accident. Mary has overcome her disability and becomes one of the most important characters in the novel because she lives in the first reality. The narrator writes: "Here, then, in this corner room of the Hotel Feldhütter in Munich, Mary fought her *aristeia,* as Homer calls the grandest and most glorious struggles of his heroes" (*Ds,* 32).

**Lord Achaz von Neudegker.** A fifteenth-century baron whose abduction and torture of several women becomes the subject of a manuscript whose first words are: "Specyfyeth of how the sorceresses were delt wyth atte Neudegck when that they were taken Anno MCCCCLXIIIJ [1464]" by his squire, **Ruodlieb von der Vläntsch.** This manuscript provides Stangeler, the historian, information for understanding the nature of obsessive behavior, which he designates as living in second reality.

**Kajetan von Schlaggenberg.** Kajetan is a novelist and writer of *Chronique Scandaleuse,* in which he develops his rather bizarre *Dicke-Damen-Doctrinar-Sexualität,* the "Theory of the Necessity of Fat Females to the Sex Life of the Superior Man Today," which he insists Geyrenhoff include in his chronicle of *die Unsrigen.* Kajetan's estrangement from his wife, Camilla von Schlaggenberg, née Schedik (Camy), gives him cause (he thinks) to construct a second reality focused on *Dicke Damen.*

**Charlotte "Quapp" von Schlaggenberg** ("Quapp," "Quappchen," "Lo," "Lotte"). Quapp is Kajetan's sister (adopted sister, as it turns out later) and heir to a rather substantial fortune left her by her real father, Captain Georg Ruthmayr. Her real mother is Countess Claire Charagiel, daughter of Baron von Neudegg. Since very few people know of this inheritance, the lawyer, Financial Counsellor Levielle, who was given a copy of Ruthmayr's will that he dictated as he was dying, attempts to defraud her of this inheritance. The primary plot line involves the discovery of this inheritance and its restoration to Quapp through the intervention of the narrator, Georg von Geyrenhoff.

**Kyrill Scolander.** Kajetan von Schlaggenberg's teacher, Scolander acts as a touchstone for Geyrenhoff's understanding of complicated financial matters related to Quapp's inheritance. Scolander represents a character who is living in first reality, and his character is presented as exactly opposite to the character of someone who is living in second reality.

**René von Stangeler.** Stangeler is a historian who has received his doctorate in history but has been unable to find a position in research or teaching. His condition—both psychological and financial—improves when a businessman, Jan Herzka, inherits a medieval castle (Castle Neudegk) in which a fifteenth-century manuscript on witchcraft is found, and he is hired to interpret this manuscript as well as to organize the castle's library.

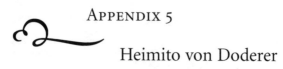

# Heimito von Doderer

Biography, with Events from *The Demons*

This biography of Heimito von Doderer is placed within a listing of events occurring in *The Demons*. Events from Doderer's life appear in boldface.

| | |
|---|---|
| 1464 | Occurrence of events in manuscript by Ruodlieb von der Vläntsch |
| 1517 | Ruodlieb von der Vläntsch writes manuscript |
| 1884 | Georg von Geyrenhoff born |
| **1896** | **Born** |
| 1900 | Geyrenhoff, aged sixteen, encounters Baroness Claire von Neudegg |
| 1914 | Captain Georg Ruthmayr dies |
| **1920–1927** | **Studied history and psychology at University of Vienna. Received doctorate in 1925.** |
| 1925 September 21 | Mary K. has accident, loses part of leg |
| 1926–1927 | Events of main story in *The Demons* occur |
| 1926 | |
| November 20 | Geyrenhoff sees Schlaggenberg on traffic island |
| November 21 | Geyrenhoff begins his chronicle of *die Unsrigen* |
| 1927 | |
| January 30 | Shooting at Schattendorf—fascists fire on communist march |
| Mid-February | Baroness Claire (Neudegg) Charagiel dies |

| | |
|---|---|
| March 3 | Ash Wednesday. Letter dated from Achaz Neudegg to Jan Herzka. |
| March 25 | Annunciation Day. Geyrenhoff (unknowingly) fires salvo at Levielle. |
| March 28 | First conversation occurs between Kajetan and Levielle (factor in Geyrenhoff's unraveling of plot to defraud Quapp of inheritance) |
| End of March | Lasch and Levielle overheard by Stangeler (factor in Geyrenhoff's unraveling of plot to defraud Quapp of inheritance) |
| Mid-April | *die Unsrigen* outing |
| May 14 | Table-tennis tea at Siebenscheins' |
| | Witches discussed, Körger's neck bothers and begins to haunt Geyrenhoff |
| | Geyrenhoff attends opera (*Der Rosenkavalier*) with Friederike |
| May 15 | Geyrenhoff awakens in a crisis |
| | Geyrenhoff visits Gürtzner-Gontard |
| | Geyrenhoff encounters Gach, who delivered Ruthmayr's will to Levielle |
| | Geyrenhoff encounters Mucki Langingen and Alfons Croix by chance |
| May 16 | Geyrenhoff stops chronicling |
| May 17 | Geyrenhoff calls Quapp about her inheritance |
| June 23 | Reception at Friederike's; Geyrenhoff confronts Levielle here |
| June 25 | Geyrenhoff goes to tea alone at Friederike's |
| July 5 | Trial of Schattendorf killers |
| July 15 | Imre Gyurkicz killed |
| | Geyrenhoff to Gürtzner-Gontard's for breakfast, 9:00 a.m. |
| | Geyrenhoff to Friederike's, 5:00 p.m. |
| | Quapp to Friederike's, 6:00 p.m. |
| Late Summer | Schlaggenberg returns from London where he "gave up" Camy |

| | |
|---|---|
| Fall | Friederike Ruthmayr and Georg von Geyrenhoff marry |
| 1929–1936 | **Wrote first part of *The Demons, Die Dämonen der Ostmark*** |
| 1933–1938 | **A member of the NSDAP, a proscribed movement.** |
| 1936–1951 | **Self-imposed period of *Gedächtnis-Distanz*** |
| 1938 | **After the Anschluss on March 13, 1938, he resigned from the NSDAP** |
| 1938–1939 | **Converted to Catholicism** |
| 1940 | Friederike dies |
| 1940–1945 | **Lieutenant in German Air Force** |
| 1945 | **Captured by British in Norway** |
| 1946 | **Returned to Vienna** |
| 1946–1950 | **Studied at the Institute for Historical Research. Became member.** |
| 1955 | Geyrenhoff finishes the novel, having put the chronicle and collected materials aside in 1927 |
| 1951–1956 | **Ended period of *Gedächtnis-Distanz*, picks up first part, *Die Dämonen der Ostmark*, revises, finishes writing *The Demons*** |
| 1962 | **Published *Die Merowinger oder Die totale Familie*** |
| 1966 | **Died** |

GLOSSARY

Note: For a fuller treatment of terms used by Voegelin, consult Sandoz, "Voegelin Glossary," in *The Collected Works of Eric Voegelin*, Volume 34, *Autobiographical Reflections: Revised Edition, with a Voegelin Glossary and Cumulative Index*.

**Anamnesis: remembrance or recollection.** In the foreword to *Anamnesis: On the Theory of History and Politics*, Voegelin places his understanding of "Anamnesis" squarely within the philosophy of order and consciousness. There he writes:

> A philosophy of order is the process through which we find the order of our existence as human beings in the order of consciousness. Plato has let this philosophy be dominated by the symbol of "Anamnesis," remembrance. Remembered, however, will be what has been forgotten; and we remember the forgotten—sometimes with considerable travail—because it should not remain forgotten. The culpably forgotten will be brought to the presence of knowledge through remembrance, and in the tension to knowledge oblivion reveals itself as the state of non-knowledge, of the *agnoia* of the soul in the Platonic sense. Knowledge and non-knowledge are states of existential order and disorder. What has been forgotten, however, can be remembered only because it is a knowledge in the mode of oblivion that through its presence in oblivion arouses the existential unrest that will urge toward its raising into the mode of knowledge. Oblivion and knowledge are modes of consciousness of which the first can be raised into the second through remembrance. Remembering is the activity of consciousness by which the forgotten, i.e., the latent knowledge in consciousness, is raised from unconsciousness into the presence of consciousness.[1]

1. Voegelin, *Anamnesis*, 36–37.

Voegelin's double empiricism, as I have called it in chapter 2, grounds his search of order in his implementation of Heraclitus's Fragment B101—"I searched into myself"—and the Socratic "Know thyself," on the one hand, and in his systematic remembering search back through the history of the human search for order to recover "what has been forgotten" but "should not remain forgotten," on the other. This anamnetic search relies upon his "participatory" imaginative reading of historical literary documents.

**Anamnetic experiments.** The **anamnetic experiments** are the results of a meditation that Voegelin conducted between late September and early November 1943, which were not published until their inclusion in *Anamnesis. Zur Theorie der Geschichte und Politik.* As Voegelin indicated to Heilman in the year of its publication, 1966, the meditation was an effort to recover "consciousness from the current theories of consciousness, especially from Phaenomenology" (*AFIL,* letter 110, June 19, 1966, p. 242). Further, the experiments were undertaken to explore the "radices of philosophizing in the biography of philosophizing consciousness, i.e., by the experiences that impel toward reflection and do so because they have excited consciousness to the 'awe' of existence."[2] The experiments consisted of Voegelin remembering the "irrupting experiences" and "the excitations" that they induced from the first ten years of his life and resulted in twenty remembered experiences published as chapter 4, "Anamnesis," in the volume of the same name.

**Apeiron: the depth.** The **apeiron,** or depth, of reality was discovered by Anaximander (c. 610–c. 547/6 BC) and symbolized as that from which all being things emerge and into which they must perish. *See* **Being in flux.**

**Apperception.** As Ellis Sandoz writes in the "Voegelin Glossary," apperception is "Leibniz's term for the introspective or reflective apprehension by the mind of its own inner states. [It] contrasts with 'perception,' which is awareness of something external."[3] Voegelin credits Doderer with formulating the refusal to apperceive or the refusal of apperception—*Apperzeptions-Verweigerung*—as the deformation of consciousness that results in the construction of second reality.

**Being in flux.** The Time of the Tale "expresses the experience of Being (that embraces all sorts of reality, the cosmos) in flux," Voegelin wrote to Heilman in August 1964 (*AFIL,* letter 103, p. 223). **Being in flux** linguistically formulates the recognition that Being continuously passes from the

---

2. Ibid., 84.
3. Sandoz, "Voegelin Glossary," 151.

"time-out-of-time" of the depth (**Apeiron**) into the space-time of the external world and back. In *The World of the Polis,* Voegelin quotes Anaximander: "The origin of things is the **Apeiron**. . . . It is necessary that things should perish into that from which they were born; for they pay one another penalty [*dike*] and compensation for their injustice [*adikia*] according to the ordinance [or: decree, *taxis*] of Time."[4] **Being in flux** symbolizes—in the Time of the Tale—the experience of having been created from the timelessness of the divine ground of existence.

**Cosmological civilizations.** In "Anxiety and Reason" and elsewhere, Voegelin writes of "societies called cosmological because their understanding of order is dominated by the primary experience of the cosmos."[5] Myths symbolize this primary cosmic experience, which arises in recognition of an ordered reality of consubstantial beings in the community of being—god, man, world and society—and issues in political and social institutions in attunement with this reality. The divine component in the cosmological style of experience is understood to be intra-cosmic instead of transcendent, as in revelatory and philosophical styles of truth.

**Critical distance.** Voegelin uses this term in "Postscript: On Paradise and Revolution," the 1971 supplement to his 1947 letter to Robert B. Heilman on Henry James's *The Turn of the Screw.* It refers to the awareness by a novelist of consciously creating a work of art rather than simply functioning as a vehicle for the expression of "inspired" or "determined" experiences. Thus the novelist as a human being living in the *metaxy* embraces the responsibility for freely, critically, and reflectively writing a novel. The term is related to Voegelin's later symbolization "reflective distance," which identifies the human capacity to reflect upon and linguistically symbolize experiences of existence as events of "conscious 'participation' in being." See chapter 1, §12, "The Symbols Reflective Distance-Remembrance-Oblivion," in *In Search of Order,* volume V of *Order and History.*

**Imagination.** For Voegelin, **imagination** is a structure in reality, just as *Nous* (Reason) is a structure in reality. The *human imagination* can be divided into the It-reality imagination and the thing-reality imagination, just as *human nous* can be divided into It-reality Nous and thing-reality nous, i.e., noetic reason and calculative reason. The human thing-reality imagination is a tool that can be used in the construction of fantasy and of second realities, just as the human thing-reality nous is a tool that can be used to deny the human It-reality Nous and to construct hells on earth. The

---

4. Voegelin, *World of the Polis,* 305–6.
5. Voegelin, "Anxiety and Reason," 58.

imagination of human consciousness can "imagine" (read "experience imaginatively") the imaginative structure of It-reality because it (human imagination) shares and participates in the imaginative structure that is part of It-reality. The reason of human consciousness can experience the rational-noetic structure of It-reality because it shares and participates in the Noetic structure of reality.

**Intentionality and Luminosity.** These terms are descriptors of structures of human consciousness. **Intentionality** may be understood as the intention to understand through reason—Aristotle's calculative reason—the objective world of external things. Thus, **intentionality** explores **thing-reality** and describes the mode of consciousness through which a modern scientist, for example, works to understand the objective world of matter. **Luminosity**, on the other hand, corresponds to, and is transparent for, **It-reality**. Although it is not really this simple, **intentionality** and **thing-reality** can be understood as the human component in the community of being, insofar as human beings are embodied creatures. **Luminosity** and **It-reality**, on the other hand, can be understood to constitute the transcendent or divine component in the community of Being. Because human consciousness exists, however, in the *metaxy,* and because human beings are composite beings who participate in all levels of being, human consciousness can access insights that are imaginative, spiritual, nonobjective, and experiential in nature.

*Metaxy.* In "Equivalences of Experience and Symbolization in History," Voegelin wrote:

> Existence has the structure of the In-Between, of the Platonic *metaxy,* and if anything is constant in the history of mankind it is the language of tension between life and death, immortality and mortality, perfection and imperfection, time and timelessness; between order and disorder, truth and untruth, sense and senselessness of existence; between *amor Dei* and *amor sui, l'âme ouverte* and *l'âme close;* between the virtues of openness toward the ground of being such as faith, love, and hope, and the vices of infolding closure such as hybris and revolt; between moods of joy and despair; and between alienation in its double meaning of alienation from the world and alienation from God.[6]

Voegelin, following and amplifying Plato, "locates" human consciousness in the *metaxy,* or the place of the "In-Between." Consciousness, paradoxically, is neither here (in the body) nor there (outside the body), but instead is here and there; it participates in both.

---

6. Voegelin, "Equivalences of Experience and Symbolization in History," 119–20.

Additionally, we find that the metaxic structure of consciousness reflects and participates in the metaxic structure of the Cosmos. Meditating upon Plato's *to pan* (the All), Voegelin writes that "the All is neither being nor not-being because it is both, the order between the opposites being persuasively mediated by the process of the psychic reality 'between' (*en meso*) being and genesis. The 'between' existence of consciousness, then, is part of the metaxic structure of the Cosmos."[7]

**Participation.** Participation (*methexis*—the Platonic participation in the Idea—and *metalepsis*—the Aristotelian mutual human-divine participation in the *Nous*) in the community of being is an essential component in Voegelin's philosophy. As a partner in the community of being, man participates in reality through his consciousness. In "The Theory of Consciousness" we read:

> Human consciousness is not a process that occurs in the world in isolation, in contact with other processes only through cognition; rather, it is based on animal, vegetative, and inorganic being, and only on this basis is it the consciousness of a human being. This structure of being seems to be the ontic premise for man's ability to transcend himself toward the world, for in none of its directions of transcending does consciousness find a level of being that is not also one on which it itself is based.[8]

This consciousness is cognitive-meditative (reflective) as well as imaginative, and the presupposition for this participation is the consubstantiality of all being and the interrelatedness of all levels of reality.

**Primary experience of the cosmos.** Ellis Sandoz defines **primary experience of the cosmos** as "Voegelin's term for what is felt and known about reality prior to philosophical or spiritual reflection that differentiates it into a 'world' and a 'beyond.' For this reason it is experienced as 'a cosmos full of gods,' a whole saturated with divine presence."[9] **Primary experience of the cosmos** also symbolizes a precognitive, almost visceral, recognition of order as it manifests itself immediately in the experiences of wonder and awe that Voegelin discerned in Aristotle's *Metaphysics* and Kant's *Critique of Practical Reason*. Moreover, in his late work Voegelin argued that both philosophy and revelation as symbolic complexes are dependent upon the **primary experience of the cosmos**, and that instead of supplanting myth, philosophy and revelation must subsume myth into their own symbolic linguistic structures.

7. Voegelin, *In Search of Order*, 106.
8. Voegelin, *Anamnesis*, 75.
9. Sandoz, "Voegelin Glossary," 175.

In "Eternal Being in Time," Voegelin identifies Plato's *Timaeus* as "a myth,"[10] and in his later discussion of *Timaeus* he writes: "Plato is struggling for a language that will optimally express the analytical movements of existential consciousness within the limits of a *fides* of the Cosmos."[11] It seems that for Voegelin a "*fides* of the Cosmos" (and what he elsewhere calls "Plato's *fides* of the Cosmos") is a linguistic equivalent to the **primary experience of the cosmos.** This section of *In Search of Order* thus brings the **primary experience of the cosmos** into the fold of the philosophical meditation. Such an inclusion has become possible with the differentiation of reflective distance as a structure of consciousness.

**Reality: nonexistent reality. Nonexistent reality** is a reality that exists, but not as existence is normally understood. The term *existence* conventionally designates the quality of being and implies that what exists must go out of existence, as in "what comes into being, must of necessity go out of being." In Sartrean existentialism, for example, existence that is understood as the bodily existence of human beings in space and time precedes the creation of essence (or meaning) by human consciousness.

Thus, **nonexistent reality** prima facie seems to be self-contradictory, for how could reality not exist? To understand the term we must embrace a paradox that lies at the heart of Voegelin's philosophy of consciousness itself. The "fact" of consciousness itself evidences a form of existing, yet not-existing simultaneously. I know that consciousness "exists," because I am herein engaged; I also know that my consciousness accompanies my body as it moves through space and endures in time, even though my consciousness "exists" in a different place, the *metaxy*, from my body, which exists in space-time. For a more complete discussion of "the field of nonexistence," see Voegelin, "Anxiety and Reason."[12]

**Reality: thing-reality,** and **It-reality.** As Voegelin continued to philosophize until his death, he symbolized his own experiences of reality and developed in his late work, especially the last volume of *Order and History*, *In Search of Order*, a clarified pair of symbols, **thing-reality** and **It-reality**. Roughly speaking, **thing-reality** corresponds to what has been understood in the earlier differentiation of revelation as immanent reality, and **It-reality** corresponds to what has been understood as transcendent reality. Furthermore, **thing-reality** designates material and existent reality and **It-reality** immaterial and nonexistent reality. Finally, while **thing-reality** includes all being things that exist in the space-time of the material world (including human bodies), **It-reality** as the transcendent divine both

10. Voegelin, *Anamnesis*, 328.
11. Voegelin, *In Search of Order*, §5, "Plato's *Timaeus*," 108.
12. Voegelin, "Anxiety and Reason," 88–91.

encompasses **thing-reality** (for **thing-reality** emerges out of the divine **Apeiron**) and orders the material **thing-reality**, human consciousness existing in the *metaxy*, and It-self (as the Platonic-Aristotelian Nous or the Judaeo Yahweh).

The earlier symbolization of the community of Being constituted of God, man, world, and society is equivalent in its comprehensiveness to the late symbolization **It-reality** that encompasses and orders the partners of the community of Being.

**Time of the Tale.** The **Time of the Tale** expresses the intersection of the timeless and time. It is both the linguistic expression of the "time" when the "timeless" irrupts into time and the "time" when time emerged from the timeless depth, the **Apeiron**.

Arendt, Hannah. Introduction to the Universal Library Edition of *The Sleepwalkers: A Trilogy,* by Hermann Broch. New York: Grosset & Dunlap, 1964.

Aristotle. *Metaphysics.* Translated by W. D. Ross. In *The Basic Works of Aristotle.* Edited and with an introduction by Richard McKeon. New York: Random House, 1941.

Bachem, Michael. *Heimito von Doderer.* Boston: Twayne Publishers, 1981.

Berry, Elaine. *Robert Frost on Writing.* New Brunswick, NJ: Rutgers University Press, 1973.

Campbell, Joseph. *The Power of Myth.* With Bill Moyers. Edited by Betty Sue Flowers. New York: Doubleday, 1988.

Camus, Albert. *The Rebel.* Translated by Anthony Bower. New York: Vintage Books, 1956.

Coles, Robert. *The Call of Stories: Teaching and the Moral Imagination.* Boston: Houghton Mifflin, 1989.

Desmond, John F. *Risen Sons: Flannery O'Connor's Vision of History.* Athens: University of Georgia Press, 1987.

Doderer, Heimito von. *The Demons.* Translated by Richard and Clara Winston. New York: Alfred A. Knopf, 1961.

——— . *Repertorium. Ein Begriefbuch von höheren und niederen Lebens-Sachen.* Edited by Dietrich Weber. Munich: Biederstein Verlag, 1969.

Dostoyevsky, Fyodor. *The Brothers Karamazov.* Translated by Constance Garnett. Edited with introduction by Manuel Komroff. New York: New American Library, 1957.

Eberhart, Richard. *Collected Poems, 1930–1986.* New York: Oxford University Press, 1988.

Embry, Charles R., ed. *Robert B. Heilman and Eric Voegelin: A Friendship in Letters, 1944–1984.* Columbia: University of Missouri Press, 2004.

Francis, Dick. *Wild Horses.* New York: Berkley Books, 2004.

Frankl, Viktor. *Man's Search for Meaning.* New York: Pocket Books, 1984.

Freeman, Kathleen, trans. *Ancilla to the Pre-Socratic Philosophers: A Complete Translation of the Fragments in Diels,* Fragmente der Vorsokratiker. Cambridge, MA: Harvard University Press, 1978.

Gordimer, Nadine. "Writing and Being." Nobel Lecture, December 7, 1991. In *Les Prix Nobel: The Nobel Prizes, 1991,* edited by Tore Frängsmyr. Stockholm: Almqvist & Wiksell International, 1992.

Heilman, Robert B. "The Freudian Reading of *The Turn of the Screw.*" *Modern Language Notes* 63 (1947): 433–45.

———. *The Professor and the Profession.* Columbia: University of Missouri Press, 1999.

Heinlein, Robert A. *Stranger in a Strange Land.* New York: Putnam, 1961.

Hesson, Elizabeth. *Twentieth Century Odyssey: A Study of Heimito von Doderer's* Die Dämonen. Columbia, SC: Camden House, 1982.

Hoye, Timothy. "Imagining Modern Japan: Natsume Soseki's First Trilogy." In *Philosophy, Literature, and Politics: Essays Honoring Ellis Sandoz,* edited by Charles R. Embry and Barry Cooper, 188–205. Columbia: University of Missouri Press, 2005.

Hosseini, Khaled. *The Kite Runner.* New York: Riverhead Books, 2003.

Hughes, Glenn. *Mystery and Myth in the Philosophy of Eric Voegelin.* Columbia: University of Missouri Press, 1993.

Kertesz, Imre. "Eureka!: The 2002 Nobel Lecture." Translated by Ivan Sanders. *World Literature Today: A Literary Quarterly of the University of Oklahoma* 77 (April–June 2003): 4–8.

Kundera, Milan. "The Depreciated Legacy of Cervantes." In *The Art of the Novel,* translated by Linda Asher. New York: Harper & Row, 1988.

Leon, Donna. *Acqua Alta.* London: Penguin Books, 1996.

McKnight, Stephen A., and Geoffrey L. Price, eds. *International and Interdisciplinary Perspectives on Eric Voegelin.* Columbia: University of Missouri Press, 1997.

Mendoza, Plinio Apuleyo, and Gabriel García Márquez. *The Fragrance of Guava.* Translated by Ann Wright. London: Verso Editions, 1983.

Nádas, Péter. "The Novelist and His Selfs." *New Hungarian Quarterly* 33, no. 127 (1992): 18.

O'Brien, Tim. *The Things They Carried.* New York: Broadway Books, 1990.

O'Connor, Flannery. *Collected Works.* New York: Library of America, 1988.

——— . *The Habit of Being: Letters of Flannery O'Connor.* Edited and with an introduction by Sally Fitzgerald. New York: Vintage Books, 1980.

——— . "Catholic Novelists and Their Readers." In *Mystery and Manners: Occasional Prose,* 169–90. Edited by Sally and Robert Fitzgerald. New York: Farrar, Straus & Giroux, 1961.

——— . "The Nature and Aim of Fiction." In *Mystery and Manners: Occasional Prose,* 63–86. Edited by Sally and Robert Fitzgerald. New York: Farrar, Straus & Giroux, 1961.

——— . "Novelist and Believer." In *Mystery and Manners: Occasional Prose,* 154–68. Edited by Sally and Robert Fitzgerald. New York: Farrar, Straus & Giroux, 1961.

——— . "On Her Own Work." In *Mystery and Manners: Occasional Prose,* 107–18. Edited by Sally and Robert Fitzgerald. New York: Farrar, Straus & Giroux, 1961.

——— . "Some Aspects of the Grotesque in Southern Fiction." In *Mystery and Manners: Occasional Prose,* 36–50. Edited by Sally and Robert Fitzgerald. New York: Farrar, Straus & Giroux, 1961.

——— . *Three by Flannery O'Connor: Wise Blood* [1962]; *The Violent Bear It Away* [1960]; *Everything That Rises Must Converge* [1965]. With an introduction by Sally Fitzgerald. New York: Signet, New American Library, 1983.

Plato. *Great Dialogues.* Translated by W. H. D. Rouse. Edited by Eric H. Warmington and Philip G. Rouse. New York: New American Library, 1956.

Polanyi, Michael. *The Tacit Dimension.* Garden City, NY: Doubleday, 1966.

Rankin, Ian. *Fleshmarket Alley.* New York: Little, Brown, 2004.

Sandoz, Ellis, ed. *Eric Voegelin's Significance for the Modern Mind.* Baton Rouge: Louisiana State University Press, 1991.

——— . *Political Apocalypse: A Study of Dostoevsky's Grand Inquisitor.* 2nd edition. Wilmington, DE: ISI Books, 2000.

——— . *The Voegelinian Revolution: A Biographical Introduction.* 2nd edition, with a new preface and epilogue by the author and a new foreword by Michael Henry. New Brunswick, N.J.: Transaction Publishers, 2000.

Sartre, Jean-Paul. *Being and Nothingness: An Essay on Phenomenological Ontology.* Translated and with an introduction by Hazel E. Barnes. New York: Philosophical Library, 1956.

Steiner, George. "Humane Literacy." In *Language and Silence: Essays on Language, Literature, and the Inhuman,* 3–11. New York: Atheneum, 1982.

——— . *Real Presences.* Chicago: University of Chicago Press, 1989.

Swift, Graham. *Waterland.* New York: Vintage Books, 1983.

Tacitus. *The Histories.* Translated by Clifford H. Moore. Loeb Classical Library. 1925. Reprint, Cambridge, MA: Harvard University Press, 1968.

Voegelin, Eric. *Anamnesis: On the Theory of History and Politics.* Edited by David Walsh. Translated by M. J. Hanak, based upon the abbreviated version originally translated by Gerhart Niemeyer. Vol. 6 of *The Collected Works of Eric Voegelin.* Columbia: University of Missouri Press, 2002.

——— . "Anxiety and Reason." In *What Is History? And Other Late Unpublished Writings,* edited with an introduction by Thomas A. Hollweck and Paul Caringella, 52–110. Vol. 28 of *The Collected Works of Eric Voegelin.* Baton Rouge: Louisiana State University Press, 1990.

——— . *Autobiographical Reflections.* Edited with an introduction by Ellis Sandoz. Baton Rouge: Louisiana State University Press, 1989.

——— . *Autobiographical Reflections.* Revised, with a Voegelin Glossary and Cumulative Index. Edited by Ellis Sandoz. Vol. 34 of *The Collected Works of Eric Voegelin.* Columbia: University of Missouri Press, 2006.

——— . "Autobiographical Statement at Age Eighty-Two." In *The Drama of Humanity and Other Miscellaneous Papers, 1939–1985,* edited with an introduction by William Petropulos and Gilbert Weiss, 432–56. Vol. 33 of *The Collected Works of Eric Voegelin.* Columbia: University of Missouri Press, 2004.

——— . "The Beginning and the Beyond: A Meditation on Truth." In *What Is History? And Other Late Unpublished Writings,* edited with an introduction by Thomas A. Hollweck and Paul Caringella, 173–232. Vol. 28 of *The Collected Works of Eric Voegelin.* Baton

Rouge: Louisiana State University Press, 1990.

————. "The Beyond and Its Parousia." In *The Drama of Humanity and Other Miscellaneous Papers, 1939–1985,* edited with an introduction by William Petropulos and Gilbert Weiss, 396–414. Vol. 33 of *The Collected Works of Eric Voegelin.* Columbia: University of Missouri Press, 2004.

————. "Conversations with Eric Voegelin at the Thomas More Institute for Adult Education in Montreal." In *The Drama of Humanity and Other Miscellaneous Papers, 1939–1985,* edited with an introduction by William Petropulos and Gilbert Weiss, 243–343. Vol. 33 of *The Collected Works of Eric Voegelin.* Columbia: University of Missouri Press, 2004.

————. "The Drama of Humanity." In *The Drama of Humanity and Other Miscellaneous Papers, 1939–1985,* edited with an introduction by William Petropulos and Gilbert Weiss, 174–242. Vol. 33 of *The Collected Works of Eric Voegelin.* Columbia: University of Missouri Press, 2004.

————. *The Ecumenic Age.* Edited with an introduction by Michael Franz. Vol. IV of *Order and History,* vol. 17 of *The Collected Works of Eric Voegelin.* Columbia: University of Missouri Press, 2000.

————. "The Eclipse of Reality." In *What Is History? And Other Late Unpublished Writings,* edited with an introduction by Thomas A. Hollweck and Paul Caringella, 111–62. Vol. 28 of *The Collected Works of Eric Voegelin.* Baton Rouge: Louisiana State University Press, 1990.

————. "Equivalences of Experience and Symbolization in History." In *Published Essays, 1966–1985,* edited with an introduction by Ellis Sandoz, 115–33. Vol. 12 of *The Collected Works of Eric Voegelin.* Baton Rouge: Louisiana State University Press, 1990.

————. "The German University and the Order of German Society: A Reconsideration of the Nazi Era." In *Published Essays, 1966–1985,* edited with an introduction by Ellis Sandoz, 1–35. Vol. 12 of *The Collected Works of Eric Voegelin.* Baton Rouge: Louisiana State University Press, 1990.

————. *Hitler and the Germans.* Translated, edited, and with an introduction by Detlev Clemens and Brendan Purcell. Vol. 31 of *The Collected Works of Eric Voegelin.* Columbia: University of Missouri Press, 1999.

————. *In Search of Order.* Edited with an introduction by Ellis Sandoz and epilogue by Jürgen Gebhardt. Vol. V of *Order and History,* vol.

18 of The *Collected Works of Eric Voegelin*. Columbia: University of Missouri Press, 2000.

———. "In Search of the Ground." In *Published Essays, 1953–1965*, edited with an introduction by Ellis Sandoz, 224–51. Vol. 11 of *The Collected Works of Eric Voegelin*. Columbia: University of Missouri Press, 2000.

———. *Israel and Revelation*. Edited with an introduction by Maurice P. Hogan. Vol. I of *Order and History*, vol. 18 of *The Collected Works of Eric Voegelin*. Columbia: University of Missouri Press, 2001.

———. *Modernity without Restraint: The Political Religions; The New Science of Politics; and Science, Politics, and Gnosticism*. Edited with an introduction by Manfred Henningsen. Vol. 5 of *The Collected Works of Eric Voegelin*. Columbia: University of Missouri Press, 2000.

———. "The Moving Soul." In *What Is History? And Other Late Unpublished Writings*, edited with an introduction by Thomas A. Hollweck and Paul Caringella, 163–72. Vol. 28 of *The Collected Works of Eric Voegelin*. Baton Rouge: Louisiana State University Press, 1990.

———. *The New Science of Politics*. Chicago: University of Chicago Press, 1952.

———. "On Debate and Existence." In *Published Essays, 1966–1985*, edited with an introduction by Ellis Sandoz, 36–51. Vol. 12 of *The Collected Works of Eric Voegelin*. Baton Rouge: Louisiana State University Press, 1990.

———. "On Hegel: A Study in Sorcery." In *Published Essays, 1966–1985*, edited with an introduction by Ellis Sandoz, 213–55. Vol. 12 of *The Collected Works of Eric Voegelin*. Baton Rouge: Louisiana State University Press, 1990.

———. *On the Form of the American Mind*. Edited by Jürgen Gebhardt. Vol. 1 of *The Collected Works of Eric Voegelin*. Baton Rouge: Louisiana State University Press, 1995.

———. *Plato and Aristotle*. Edited with an introduction by Dante Germino. Vol. III of *Order and History*, vol. 16 of *The Collected Works of Eric Voegelin*. Columbia: University of Missouri Press, 2000.

———. "Postscript: On Paradise and Revolution." Part B of Voegelin, review of *The Turn of the Screw*. *Southern Review*, n.s. 7 (1971): 25–48.

————. "Postscript: On Paradise and Revolution." In *Published Essays, 1966–1985,* edited by Ellis Sandoz, 149–71. (Part of "On Henry James's *Turn of the Screw,*" 134–71.) Vol. 12 of *The Collected Works of Eric Voegelin.* Baton Rouge: Louisiana State University Press, 1990.

————. "Wisdom and the Magic of the Extreme: A Meditation." In *Published Essays, 1966–1985,* edited with an introduction by Ellis Sandoz, 315–75. Vol. 12 of *The Collected Works of Eric Voegelin.* Baton Rouge: Louisiana State University Press, 1990.

————. *The World of the Polis.* Edited with an introduction by Athanasios Moulakis. Vol. II of *Order and History,* vol. 15 of *The Collected Works of Eric Voegelin.* Columbia: University of Missouri Press, 2000.

Wood, Ralph C. *Flannery O'Connor and the Christ-Haunted South.* Grand Rapids, MI: William B. Eerdmans, 2004.

INDEX

 CREDITS

Acknowledgment is made as follows for permission to quote from copyrighted material:

From *The Demons, Vol. I and II,* by Heimito von Doderer, translated by Richard and Clara Winston, copyright © 1961 and renewed 1989 by Alfred A. Knopf, a division of Random House, Inc. Used by permission of Alfred A. Knopf, a division of Random House, Inc.

Three lines from "Birth and Death," p. 226 from *Collected Poems, 1930–1986,* by Richard Eberhart. Used by permission of Oxford University Press, Inc.

Quotations from Eric Voegelin reprinted from *Robert B. Heilman and Eric Voegelin: A Friendship in Letters, 1944–1984,* ed. Charles R. Embry, by permission of University of Missouri Press. Copyright © 2004 by the Curators of the University of Missouri.

The following are reprinted by permission of Farrar, Straus and Giroux, LLC: Excerpts from *Mystery and Manners,* by Flannery O'Connor, edited by Sally and Robert Fitzgerald. Copyright © 1969 by the Estate of Mary Flannery O'Connor. Excerpts from *The Violent Bear It Away,* by Flannery O'Connor. Copyright © 1960 by Flannery O'Connor. Renewed copyright © 1988 by Regina O'Connor. Excerpts from *Wise Blood,* by Flannery O'Connor. Copyright © 1962 by Flannery O'Connor. Copyright renewed 1990 by Regina O'Connor. Excerpts from *The Habit of Being: Letters of Flannery O'Connor,* edited by Sally Fitzgerald. Copyright © 1979 by Regina O'Connor.

The following are reprinted by permission of the Estate of Flannery O'Connor via Harold Matson Co., Inc.: *Mystery and Manners* © 1969 by The Estate of Mary Flannery O'Connor. *The Violent Bear It Away* ©1960 by Flannery O'Connor. Copyright renewed 1988 by Regina O'Connor. *Wise Blood* © 1962 by Flannery O'Connor. Copyright renewed 1990 by Regina O'Connor. *The Habit of Being: Letters of Flannery O'Connor,* edited by Sally Fitzgerald, © 1979 by Regina O'Connor.

## ABOUT THE AUTHOR

Photo by Polly Detels

Charles R. Embry is Professor Emeritus of Political Philosophy at Texas A&M University–Commerce. He is a co-author (with Glenn Hughes) of *The Eric Voegelin Reader* and is the editor of three volumes in the Eric Voegelin Institute Series in Political Philosophy, all published by the University of Missouri Press. He is also the co-editor (with Glenn Hughes) of *The Timelessness of Proust: Reflections on* In Search of Lost Time. He lives in Bellingham, Washington.